RICOCHET THROUGH LIFE

HOW TO WEAVE YOUR WAY
THROUGH A BRAIN TUMOR

BY TONI SEYMOUR

Thanks for being part of my healing team

Toni

Dedication Page

First and foremost I want to thank my parents for raising me with enough grit and determination to make it through my brain tumor journey. I could not have made it through this if I had not had the upbringing that I did. Many people told me after my surgeries, I could not have gone through what you did.

Next I'd like to thank my family and husband. You were all fabulous members of my team and did a lot of heavy mental lifting for me. You kept my spirits up and my body moving forward. Thank you, thank you, thank you for all your prayers, positive thoughts, emails, and phone calls (even when I couldn't talk loud enough for you to hear my thank yous!) My husband was an enduring strength for me throughout this journey and the rock I continue to lean on.

The doctors, nurses and staff at UCSF have been awesome. Dr. Parsa, Neurosurgeon, UCSF, Dr. Barani, Radiology/Oncology, UCSF, Dr. Plesh, Dental, UCSF, Dr. Hoyt, Neuro

Ophthalmologist, Dr. Blevins, Neuro
Endocrinologist. Outside of UCSF is Dr.
Snape, Neuro Gastroenterologist, Sutter
Pacific Medical Center, Dr. Martin Rossman,
MD/Acupuncture, Elizabeth Seymour, massage
and cranial/sacral work, Aki, Shiatsu
Center, Shiatsu massage (Portland, OR),
David Tircuit, Acupuncture and Que Gung
(Portland, OR), and my local gym, Body
Kinetics through my yoga class with Beth
Kraft and my core exercise class with
Roberta Kralj. They came from locations all
over the world, to study here, to practice
here, and to eventually intersect with my
world. I'm so grateful they all did.

A shout out to St. Anthony's Church in
Novato, CA. Your prayer group, I have no
doubt, has been instrumental to my healing.
Thanks for being on the team.

A huge thank you to Frank Borsellino
for transcribing my files. I had come to a
standstill after writing about 20 pages.
Finally, realizing I could talk into an MP3
player while I walked my 2 miles per day, I
found Frank, via my Mom, who would
transcribe what I talked into the player.

Not sure I could have ever finished the book without you Frank. Thank you so much.

Thanks to Birgitte Necessary for copyediting the entire book. Who knew I used the words so and just so often!

Everyone all over the world: Turkey, Salt Lake City, and wherever else you were praying for me…..thank you. I know it made a difference. I could feel it wash through me.

Note:

Any of my medical conditions I speak about in the book are from my understanding of what was told to me by my docs or my practitioner. These are not meant to be exact, simply my understanding, in lay terms, of what had happened, what was going to happen, would might or could happen, and what did happen.

Chapter 1 Life Happens

"People don't need an explanation of their lives as much as they need an experience of being alive." —Joseph Campbell

I am a weaver. I am a brain tumor survivor and this is my story. It begins in July, 2005. We are preparing for my son's wedding on the Oregon coast. We couldn't have been happier about this upcoming event, even if it brought with it the usual amount of stress.

In early July, while working at my desk in our home office, my husband informed me that my right eye was drooping slightly. I had also noticed a minor amount of tingling on the right side of my face.

My husband, Don, is a physician, so he determined rather quickly that I was not having a stroke (I should hope not, I was only 54). His best guess was Bell's palsy, which can be brought on by stress. We got an anti-viral drug prescription and the symptoms disappeared almost immediately. Diagnosis and treatment seemed to be a match, so we didn't give it another thought.

Don did tell me that Bell's palsy can recur. Sure enough, every 6 months or so the eye would droop and the fuzziness in the right cheek would return. Back on the anti-viral I went, and away went the symptoms. Until July of 2009.

The Bell's palsy symptoms returned, but this time the anti-viral drug had no effect. The symptoms remained. I called my Ear, Nose, and Throat doctor, Dr. Win Hall, thinking maybe it could be a sinus infection. He would not even come to the phone. The message he sent back through his nurse: See a neurologist *now*.

"No," I said, "it's probably just sinus."

"Neurologist, *now*." She said.

This seemed like overkill so I attempted to argue with her a bit, but she was very insistent.

"Hang up the phone and call a neurologist immediately."

So on July 28, 2009, Don and I went into San Francisco to see a Neurologist, Dr. Kathy Madison. We explained to her our course of action for the past 4 years and she agreed, most likely Bell's palsy, especially since the anti-viral took away the symptoms each time. She wanted to try a different anti-viral and also recommended acupuncture. We thanked her and got up.

As we opened the door to leave, she suggested that, just to cover all bases, we should do an MRI of my brain. That made sense so we agreed.

She wrote up the order and sent us to have it done. We were most anxious to just get the clean bill of health from the scan and then proceed from there.

While waiting for the results, we played with another symptom reliever; massive doses of Vitamin C, three or four times a day. Each time I drank it, powered and put into soda, the symptoms went away. But they stayed away only for a few hours, so I'd repeat the Vitamin C and gone were the symptoms. No one has ever been able to explain how the anti-viral and Vitamin C were able to take away the drooping eye and fuzziness on the right side of my face.

Chapter 2 The Diagnosis

As I was leaving the house on the morning of the 29th of July for my daily two mile walk, the e-fax results came into my computer for the brain MRI. I was alone at the time. Don was at morning mass, so I double clicked on the PDF file and opened the scan results.

Lots of medical gibberish appeared, but one word stood out: *Meningioma*. That didn't sound like something I wanted in my head. I Googled it.

From what I could tell, I had a brain tumor. That seemed really unrealistic to me. Wouldn't I have all kinds of whacked out symptoms if I had a brain tumor? I printed out the results and headed out the door, forwarding a copy to my new acupuncturist, who I was scheduled to see for the first time that morning.

As I drove out of our neighborhood, Don drove in. I waved him down and took over the fax to him. I have never seen a person's face drop the way his did. He didn't need to speak. I knew instantly that I did in fact have a brain tumor.

"I have a brain tumor don't I?"

"Yes," he answered, "and it appears to be quite large." He added that he didn't really know much about meningiomas. We headed back to the house to research our next move. I think we were both too stunned by the unexpected diagnosis to react with more than sinking hearts. Brain tumor as a diagnosis had never crossed either of our minds. I was active, intelligent, and involved in life. Shouldn't that mean I also had a well-functioning brain?

We did a little research on our home computers before heading out to see my acupuncturist, Dr. Marty Rossman. Marty was both a western medical MD, as well as an acupuncturist. He had known my husband for many years. By the time we arrived, Dr. Rossman had done some research on his own and determined that this type of brain tumor is rarely cancerous. That possibility

had not yet entered my realm of reality
but, it was certainly comforting to hear.

At this point my stoicism faded and
the tears began. My main question for these
two men was how to tell my 84-year old
parents that I had a brain tumor without
them having a heart attack on the spot. Dr.
Rossman said I just needed to tell it
straight. I'd probably be surprised how
they handled it, and how supportive they
would be.

Ugh! And my son and his wife with my
2 year old grandchild. And my husband's 6
children and those 6 grandchildren. How do
I tell any of them… or anyone, friends,
loved ones…? How do you just blurt this
out?

One by one, I made the calls and sent
out the emails. Of course everyone
concerned was supportive. I have always
found it interesting that on that crucial
day of discovering I had a brain tumor, my
main concern was how to tell my parents.

I seemed to be handling it well; sleeping well, eating well, continuing to work from our home office.

Life continued on for heaven's sake and I still put one foot in front of the other and kept truckin'. I never felt like I was in denial over what was happening. It seemed pointless to get depressed or down. I looked at it as a matter of getting on with a solution to this problem.

Also, "Brain Tumor" seemed like such a HUGE concept. No pun intended but how do you get your brain around that? Doctors were going to slice open my head and take stuff out. Who has that done? Certainly no one I knew. I think the whole concept of it was just too much to grasp. Maybe breaking it up into pieces was a good way to deal with the magnitude of it all.

Don called on his colleagues in the medical field to determine the top medical facility for this type of brain tumor and which doctor I should see. We were ready, willing, and able to fly me anywhere in the world to get this tumor out of my head.

They all came back with the same answer: University of California, San Francisco (UCSF) Brain Tumor Clinic. The neurosurgeon they recommended was Dr. Andrew Parsa.

We checked out Dr. Parsa online. He had amazing credentials. Years ago, a Dr. Charlie Wilson was in charge of setting up the Brain Tumor Clinic at UCSF. He told the University he would do it only if he could set up the best facility in the world, in order to attract the top neurosurgeons worldwide. It worked. Brain tumor is the number one diagnosis of anyone admitted to the hospital at UCSF, and has been for a long time. They have clearly earned a stellar reputation in this field of medicine.

After hearing the size of my tumor, Dr. Parsa's assistant, E. J., agreed to get us in immediately. Here is a copy of the email that was sent out to everyone on Aug. 4, 2009 after meeting Dr. Parsa:

> "Wow. The doctor was awesome. He leaned forward, looked me in the eye and said "I do this surgery

all the time. I can absolutely
take out this tumor. "

What a great relief that he was
certain they could get it out and
that it was not cancer.
Meningiomas are rarely cancerous.

Just wanting to get going with
this. There are places in the
world I need to see still!

Love to everyone. Thank you so
much for all the encouragement!

—T

This meeting with Dr. Parsa marked the
first time that we found out my tumor was
even operable. Until then, we didn't know
if my MRI diagnosis was a death sentence or
if there were options available to me. The
appointment with Dr. Parsa answered a lot
questions. And how convenient that we lived
just on the other side of the Golden Gate
Bridge from UCSF. We were willing to go
anywhere in the world and all we had to do
was drive 45 minutes into the city of San
Francisco.

After the meeting we rushed downstairs
and outside the hospital, turned on our
cell phones, and I shout, "Okay, you call
my Dad and Kathy (Don's daughter). I'll
call my Mom and Jasen. We just kept telling
everyone we could reach that the next step
was surgery. They could get the tumor out.
A plan was now in place. If I could survive
two 10-hour surgeries, I would have a life
to live and friends and family to continue
to love and I could travel the world.

Chapter 3 Action Plan

"Faith is taking the first step even when you don't see the whole staircase." –Martin Luther King, Jr.

Now I needed my own personal plan of action. My surgery dates were set for September 23 and October 28, and each surgery would take ten hours. How does one prepare for that? Mentally I needed to get my head together and get focused.

For starters, I still had my second surgeon to visit. There would be two surgeons during each surgery. Dr. Parsa would remove the tumor and Dr. Cheung would protect my optical and auditory nerves as they would need to be moved and lifted during surgery. Dr. Cheung was a specialist in this regard, and they would not proceed with the surgery until I had met him.

Waiting for my surgery was not without a bit of stress. This email went out on 8/11/2009:

No Surgery Date yet.
So no surgery date yet. Don talked with the office of the ENT

surgeon. The lady at first said early this month. They chatted longer until Don saw an opening, then stressed how important Dr. Parsa thought it was that I get surgery sooner rather than later. —T

The receptionist pulled my chart that had been faxed from Dr. Parsa's office. When she looked at the chart and saw that how large the tumor was, she moved my file to the top of the stack. Still, Dr. Cheung was on vacation would not be back until Monday.

But she also said that Dr. Cheung was not out of town and often popped in to his office. If he did, she would show him my case. That was all we could do for the moment. It appeared as if my surgery would be scheduled, at the latest early next month but could be as early as next week.

The stress of it all began to take an emotional toll. On August 25, 2009 I sent the following email:

Met with the ENT surgeon yesterday. Really, really nice man. He spent a lot of time with us. Answered many of our questions.

He also said if it was his family member he would have them do the surgery. He did say that there is a 50/50 chance I will lose hearing in my right ear. So that just means I'm pole vaulting to age 80 as far as hearing goes. Also 50/50 chance that the parts of my face that experience numbness will stay that way.

He said as far as the tumor wrapping around the carotid artery… they don't actually try and get all of that off. He said they can cut it at each end and then it has no blood supply. So a small piece of it will just lay dead on the artery.

He said for this type of tumor there are not seizures. Some headaches. And I may need rehab to get all limbs up and running again, but that my quality of life should remain as it is except for the hearing and maybe facial symptoms.

So all pretty good news.

Got home from that visit and my stomach clamped down. Pain was unrelenting. I think all of this finally hit home. Lasted at home for about 2 hours in horrible pain...then we went to the emergency room.

After several shots of morphine I didn't care where I was. Did all kinds of testing and all looked fine. So just extreme upper GI symptoms. Moved me to a room around midnight and gave me Ambien to sleep. Sometime during the night the pain released and went away.

Have now slept all day and am now beginning to feel pretty rested. Not eating much yet but imagine I'll try a few light foods tomorrow.

Pretty scary night. At times my whole body was vibrating. We were in touch with the hospital where surgery will be done so they were ready for me if I had to go into surgery. All the symptoms I've had since this started where magnified ten times last night.

But it appears none of it was brain related, except maybe mentally...by me.

Am recovering and moving onward and upward. That was a dry run for all of us here and we found a few gaps so we'll plug those now and move along.—T

The following is a better description of what went on the afternoon I went into the Emergency Room. Upon returning home from the visit with Dr. Cheung, we had lunch and walked our dogs. My mom and stepfather were living with us at the time. They had decided to move to Novato before we knew anything about the tumor. Lucky for us, we now had built in dog watchers.

As my mom and I returned home from walking the dogs, I felt as if I was going to vomit. I went into the bedroom just to rest for a bit and see if I couldn't get my stomach to settle down. Instead, the lower abdominal area just kept getting more and more painful. Finally I did vomit, but it did not resolve the pain issue.

When Don came to look in on me, I was moaning in pain. I've never moaned from pain in my life—I have a very high pain threshold, so he knew it had to be intense.

Off to the ER we went, only to experience the same old song and dance there, sit down, fill out lengthy forms, and wait. There were three or four other people ahead of us, so I knew I was in for a long wait.

I wasn't aware of how loudly I was moaning, while rocking back and forth. Everyone was looking at me. The pain was super intense. The hospital staff decided to forget the forms and rushed me in. After a cursory exam and brief explanation from Don on my recent diagnosis of the brain tumor, I was put on a morphine drip.

What I didn't know or was in too much pain to understand, was that the doctors at this local hospital, plus the ones they had reached out to at UCSF, were concerned that, due to its size, the tumor might be herniating into the spinal column. In lay language: instant death. Doctors already knew the brain stem was being shoved sideways by the tumor. What I needed at

this point was another MRI to compare with
the one already done to determine if this
was the case.

Don called my mom, walked her through
finding our copy of the MRI and asked her
to bring it to the hospital. Since she had
only lived in Novato for a matter of days,
she had no idea where the hospital was. Don
asked her if she could go across the street
and ask our neighbor, Tony, to bring it to
the hospital instead. She looked out the
front window in time to see Tony pulling
out of his driveway.

Throwing down the phone, she ran out
the front door yelling at Tony, and waving
her arms. She managed to get his attention
and he stopped. She explained the situation
and he brought the previous MRI results to
the hospital.

The local hospital had no one on staff
in the evening to read the MRI I needed
now, so they contacted a technician in
Australia. This Australian technician would
have both results. Their response was that

there seemed to be no change in the tumor size or location.

Don got on the phone with UCSF Neurosurgery, explained what was happening and had them compare their MRI with the new one. They too agreed that they saw no changes.

In the meantime, I'd received so much morphine that Don, sitting at my bedside in the ER, had to keep nudging me to get me to breathe. Many times, as he sat there, I just stopped. Finally, I received enough morphine to mask the pain, and I was able to sleep.

We'd entered the ER around six o'clock in the evening and I sent Don home around one o'clock in the morning. At two in the morning I was moved to another room where I stayed until the next day when I was released. No one ever knew exactly what happened.

This email went out on 8/12/2009

Surgery Date

Date for the first surgery is Sept. 23. They schedule the second one after first one is done....about 12 days later.

I couldn't think of any good reasons why I should be excited about my surgery being so far off until I called my Dad. He said it meant my surgeon was in high demand. I wouldn't want a surgeon that was available tomorrow.

I would certainly be ready to go by September 23rd.

We were taking this in logical steps, processing each step as we went and making decisions as needed. —T

I sent another email out on 8/21/2009 explaining the process of the brain tumor surgery:

Stealth MRI

So the afternoon before surgery (September 22) they'll be doing this Stealth MRI, with fiducial markers placed on my head. I think maybe I can be 'beamed up' at that point!

So amazing what they can do now:

Computerized "Stealth System" for Brain Surgery

Virtual brain surgery-using a computer to plan a surgical approach and tell the surgeon where to operate. Sounds like "Star Wars" technology. Technology is known as Frameless Stereotaxy using the STEALTH System.

Here's the url for how it works. http://www.neurospinewi.com/newsletters/stealthsystem.html.—T

One of my better early decisions was getting involved in alternative medicine, specifically acupuncture, with Dr. Martin Rossman. I am fortunate that Dr. Rossman is one of the leading clinicians in Guided Imagery. I had long been a fan of visualization, but Guided imagery is different, something I didn't realize until I discovered Dr. Rossman.

I had coached a high school soccer team in the 80's and had used visualization successfully with them. Many told me they carried that tool with them into their adult life.

I loaded Dr. Rossman's "Healing Through Guided Imagery" CD onto my iPhone and away I went. I could sink into his voice and get into the imagery immediately. He had a special guided imagery, "Preparing for Surgery," that I listened to twice a day, once in the afternoon and again as I was falling asleep at night.

With this technique, I felt well on my way to preparing myself for my surgeries, which was a good thing as my surgery date was moved up.

Email of 8/26/2009

Surgery Date Moved Up

Got a call today. My surgery date has been moved up to September 2nd. Apparently the ENT surgeon spoke with the neurosurgeon and they both felt the surgery should be sooner rather than later.

I'm rushing around now trying to tie up any loose ends. Almost have

that finished. Meeting on Monday
with the Prepare Team who will
walk me thru this whole process.
Then I go in on Tuesday for the
Stealth MRI, with surgery on Wed.

So glad I don't have to wait until
the 23rd. The ENT doctor told us
the other day that once they go
into surgery there will be no
messages coming out to family
until around 5pm the day of
surgery. That would be the soonest
you will hear anything.—T

Because of the size of the tumor, Don
was very worried about it herniating. He
had literally picked up the phone to call
my surgical team when they called him

He then called me and broke the "great
news." Not so great news to me. "But I'm
not ready," was my response. I felt I had
not done sufficient imagery to prepare my
mind and body for the surgery. Don
explained everyone's concern about the
tumor herniating and my possible death, so
I agreed, reluctantly, to move the date to
September 2nd. But only if I could be home

from the hospital by Sunday, for the
opening of the NFL football season!

Chapter 4 Who is Floating in My Boat?

"I will not let anyone walk through my mind with their dirty feet." —Mahatma Gandhi

"So throw off the bow lines. Sail away from the safe harbor. Catch the Trade Winds in your sails. Explore. Dream. Discover." —-Mark Twain

I learned from a previous illness, an unexplained heart attack in 1986 at age 35, that if you care-take those around you when you are recovering, it can become draining very quickly.

Everyone starts pulling and tugging on you because they don't know what to do with their feelings about your condition. It's a very natural human reaction on their part.

How many times have we all said, "I'm so sorry this happened to you." If you reflect on that statement, you realize it's a negative sentiment that you've just dumped into the lap of the person dealing with their illness. Much better to say, "How can I help? Can I cook some meals for you, clean your house, take you to doctor appts…..how best can I help you at this time?"

Having been through the experience once, I now had the wisdom to know that I was going to choose who got to be on my boat and surround me with love, prayer, and healing energy. I couldn't be the one to hold their hand through this. I was going to need to gather all my energy to bolster my health, my mood, and my energy to get through these surgeries.

I didn't throw many friends overboard, but some had to tread water until I was ready to deal with them. I know they meant well, but meaning well wasn't going to keep me strong and focused on my health and wellness during this time. Now was the time for my hand to be held, not for me to hold the hand of those who felt sorry for me.

Take control of those around you instead of letting them take control of you. You don't need energy vampires near you when you're healing from surgery. You need empathy, not sympathy. Sympathy will bring you down.

In an attempt to make sure our friends and family understood what I was about to go through, Don and I went around to each family member that lived locally and met with them so they could ask us any questions or discuss any concerns they might have.

But also, we wanted them to see that we were not afraid. I was not sitting around shaking in my boots. I had done all the proper up-front work in finding good doctors, getting our questions answered, done tons of visualization and guided imagery so that both Don and I were as prepared as we could be.

That's mostly what we wanted them to see. That we were ready to take this head on. Giddy up!

In my guided imagery, I pictured a boat. And on the boat were all the people who supported my healing. Those that subtracted from the healing and sucked energy from me, I handed a life preserver to them and watched them jump overboard to tread water.

There was one family member I had thrown off my boat that everyone encouraged me to meet with before the surgeries.

Initially, when I emailed her about the tumor, I got an email back that said, "Oh No. This is terrible." As soon as I opened her email, my body language kicked in and I backed away from my monitor. I knew this response was not good going into my brain. I needed to stay away from this kind of thinking. I completely understood her reaction, but I had to throw her off the boat to keep my thinking clear, positive and on track.

At this point, I handed over all communication with her, phone, email, and text to Don. He was my buffer. He'd handle the folks not on my boat so they'd not have access to me.

I finally decided, in case I should die, that I didn't want to leave unfinished business.

A couple of days before the surgery, Elizabeth and I met for tea. After time and reflection, she was completely upbeat and supportive. Two years later she had life threatening surgery. I had set the example for her and she built her own boat of loving, supportive people.

I set up a group email so I could update everyone at once about my condition. Even the ones treading water were included in the group email, but if they emailed back I didn't read them. I just deleted them. All others I read as I knew they would support my journey with this brain tumor.

We also found it helpful to give our children and parents jobs to do while I was in the hospital. We asked for no visitors at the hospital. I was in the hospital to recover and get home, not for social visits or worse, from someone visiting that might be coming down with a cold or the flu. We knew family wanted to see me, but they all understood it was better if I concentrated on my healing.

My neurosurgeon, Dr. Parsa, actually asked that family not come and sit in the waiting room during surgery. He said it was a small room and 10 hours would be a long time to sit and wait. We asked everyone to stay home.

Don set up a phone tree so that he only needed to call a handful of people after I was out of surgery. They in turn called a small group of people. That way everyone was kept in the loop, but Don didn't have to spend hours doing it. He would call his daughter Kathy and she would call all of her brothers and sisters.

One daughter, Kim, was in charge of my personal and business email. She sent out the group email while I was in the hospital and kept every one updated that way.

Kathy made sure we had food in the house once I got home from the hospital as we had forgotten to consider that. I think we thought I'd be able to eat anything, but as it turned out, I needed only fluids and mushy food (yogurt, cottage cheese, etc.). Kathy also packaged and shipped our books for us so we could continue selling online during the surgeries. Since my mom was at our house dog sitting, she would pull the books that sold from our book room and then Kathy could ship it. They made a good team.

Allison was in charge of texting me while I was at the hospital. I knew I'd be restless just lying there every day. It always brought a smile to my lips when the text came in. Allison, Jasen and Austen also made me delicious chocolate chip cookies that arrived each time I was released from the hospital.

My last night at home, after dark, I took our dogs into the back yard for their last call, looked up at the stars, raised both arms straight up to the sky and released the entire upcoming event to the universe. It was out of my hands now and off my shoulders. I had done all I could, mentally and physically, to prepare myself for the surgery. We'd found the best doctors in the world, the best surgical facility in the world, I'd done tons of guided imagery to prepare my mind and body for surgery, and had surrounded myself with

love, prayer and positive energy from
friends and family all over the world.

There was nothing left for me to do
but relax and move forward.

Chapter 5 Am I Alive?

"Anyone who doesn't believe in miracles is not a realist."
—David Ben-Gurion.

Email from Kim just prior to surgery:

Let the Force Be With You!

Let the surgery begin. Don, Jasen and I spent the night in a hotel before my surgery. Only Don was allowed in the waiting room. Jasen flew home to Portland the morning of the surgery but he really wanted to be with us the night before. Don suggested that Jasen might not want to see me when I came out of surgery, so he agreed to come back after I returned home from the hospital and be our chef for a couple of days.

I don't remember much about the morning of surgery. They had shaved off hair on my scalp and put fiducials on my head the day before. I had to leave them on overnight, showering with a shower cap. The fiducials are used with specialized software during surgery to line up the operating tools.

I pictured the process much like a video game. The neurosurgeon gets the markers all lined up and shoot (cut) away. I felt that the procedure was a little less grim if I pictured it like that, rather than thinking of them slicing open my head.

I do remember laying on the gurney and Don standing beside me. The prep team gave me something to relax and that's it. I remember the gurney being wheeled out of the bay I was in, around a corner, and nothing else.

Email sent on 9/2/2009

Update on Toni's surgery

Hi Everyone,

Toni asked me to update you via email when news came in. Toni is out of surgery. It couldn't have gone better, the doctors said. They got almost all of the tumor out that was pressing on the brain stem, and are so pleased with the

surgery they may wake her tonight
instead of tomorrow.

Keep sending your good thoughts,
they're working!

Kim

(From Toni's email)

My first memory after the surgery was
being in Intensive Care and vomiting again
and again. Any time there was any sort of
movement, even movement of the blanket
covering me, it set off more vomiting. UGH!

Then I remember dozing and someone
took my hand. I knew immediately it was
Don. I opened my eyes, but everything was
fuzzy. I remember saying, "Am I'm alive?"
He said. "Yes, you're alive."

I wasn't sure if it was real, a dream
or maybe I was looking down from Heaven and
imagining it all. After that I don't
remember much else except him leaving and
we telling each other "I love you."

My care nurse kept pumping in anti-
nausea drugs and finally my urge to vomit

stopped. The doctors wanted a post-surgery MRI, but I remember the care nurse going to bat for me over and over, and saying, "You can wait. I'm not sending her into an MRI when she's vomiting like this. You just have to wait until it's under control." In my mind, as I was dozing, I kept thanking her for watching out for me. I'm claustrophobic and MRI's are hard for me, even without the constant vomiting.

Finally, finally, finally, after many hours, it was time for me to leave intensive care. The head floor nurse of the neurosurgery unit was a woman named Lisa. She had been over several times to check on me in intensive care. I was supposed to have been moved, literally hours before.

They notified Lisa that I was on my way over. They transferred me to the gurney without me feeling nauseous and I was wheeled to the neurosurgery recovery floor. As we passed the nurses' station, Lisa came out from behind the counter, and shouted at everybody in the nurses' station, "I'm going to lunch. It's a beautiful day outside. This is our new patient. The

orderly's going to put her in her room.
Somebody get down there and take care of
her." And off she went to lunch.

The orderly took me into the room, got
me into bed, brought the little stand over
that they put the food on, and put a paper
cup there, no water, just a paper cup. Then
he adjusted my bed so I was comfortable,
and left. On his way out, he shut the door.
That's where I was for the next hour.
Nobody knew I was in there and Lisa was at
lunch. The orderly had never put the call
button close enough for me to reach. I
could look over the side of the bed and see
it but try as I might, I couldn't reach it.
I had very specific instructions: "Do not
get out of bed!" The only thing I could do
was take my paper cup and bang it on the
tray (clearly a paper cup doesn't make that
much noise) hoping that somebody on the
other side of the door might wonder what
the heck was going on. The phone in the
room was also outside my reach, and I
didn't have my I-phone with me yet; my
husband was bringing it when he came back.

He was at lunch also. I laid there for the next hour.

Finally, Lisa showed up. None of this was her fault. She had made sure that everybody knew I was coming, showed me to them as I passed the nurses' station, and still the ball got dropped. Because nobody picked it up, I ended up in my room by myself, a little bit scared, needing to go to the bathroom, and unable to reach out to anyone.

Lisa gave everybody grief about how they had left me alone, and got me hooked up to the monitors, got me water, got me the nurses' call button, got me a bedpan, and I was good to go. No damage done. Shortly after that, my husband showed up and stayed the rest of the afternoon. I dozed off and on. I was on heavy doses of steroids so that my brain stem and brain wouldn't swell from the surgery, as they had literally lifted up sections of my brain to get at tumor beneath.

Email sent on 9/3/2009

Got a text at 10:20pm last night:
"Toni is awake and alert! Able to
move extremities and even smiled."

Will email once I hear more.—K

(From Toni's email)

Email sent on 9/3/2012

More updates from throughout the
day...

Hi Everyone,

I've been away from my computer
all day. Now that I'm home, wanted
to share the texts from Don (Dad)
that were received throughout the
day.

 10am text:

Toni doing very well. Much more
alert, meds and some food by
mouth, much dozing. Routine MRI
this am. All ok. Bigger smile from
her this am.

 2:30pm text:

Same as this am

 7:15pm

Toni stood at bedside this afternoon. Pain much less - still very exhausted. Much more alert and smiles. Your love and supporting thoughts are working!!
—K

(From Toni's email)

Email sent 9/4/2009

Update and keep the good thoughts coming....

Hi Everyone,

Just got more detailed information... I am and have been sharing everything as I receive it.

Toni's right ear had hearing loss from the surgery and has been improving every day. She also has double vision in both eyes. As the nerves heal and repair, the hope is they will begin to improve. No pain today! Talking at a whisper. Walking with a walker.

Toni appears to be improving physically better than expected. They may even send her home to recuperate instead of sending her to the rehabilitation hospital.

It's still pretty early in her recovery so keep those thoughts and prayers coming. She told me before all of this that they mean the world to her!

With love,

Kim (from Toni's email)

It was almost impossible to sleep on steroids. I'm not exactly sure what they do to you but sleep is really hard to attain. I was able to doze off and on that afternoon. I got my iPhone back. It was son's wife Allison's job to text me so that I didn't just lay there completely bored in the hospital. Within 24 hours of having surgery, I'm sitting in my hospital bed, texting. If somebody had told me you could have brain surgery and be texting within the next 24 hours, I would have thought they were nuts. But I was completely coherent and knew that I needed to get the brain working. I figured this was a good way to do it.

That first night, when sleep wouldn't come, I laid in bed designing rugs in my head. I'm a weaver, and so I thought about how I would weave them and what colors I would make them, in an attempt to keep my brain moving and sparking, and everything reconnecting that maybe got a little disconnected.

I did have a lot of problems eating and drinking. I also had no voice as my vocal chords (we found out later) were paralyzed. We weren't not sure if that was from being tubed for ten hours, or if it was just the result of moving nerves around, but I ended up with no voice for the next eight months. I could only whisper. Talking to anybody on the phone was almost out of the question as they couldn't hear me. But I could text, and I could e-mail, and Kim, our daughter, was sending out e-mails to everyone on my group list, updating them and letting them know how I was doing.

One afternoon, maybe day two, I was resting in bed and an amazing, tingling peaceful feeling just washed through me. There was no doubt in my mind that because of all the people praying for me, all the people thinking positive thoughts and sending positive energy, that it had all just washed through me. There was no doubt in my mind that about what I had felt. I had turned this entire process over to the universe and the universe said, "We heard you and we're here for you."

On the second day after surgery, Dr. Parsa brought his children on rounds. How refreshing. Since much of my adult life had involved teaching kids, it always brought energy to me being around young people. I thought he was brilliant to do this, both so they could see all of us in our various stages of recovery, and also so we could see them and know that the world outside our hospital room was continuing on. As an aside, about a year later as we left a follow-up appointment with Dr. Parsa, I had the opportunity to tell him how wonderful that experience had been and how much it meant to me. He was delighted to hear it. He said some of his fellow doctors felt he should not be doing that, so he was glad to know of the impact it had on me.

The email blasts and texting had succeeded in letting everybody know what was going on; I had survived and was doing well. But because my vocal chords were paralyzed and my esophagus wasn't working correctly, eating and swallowing became a huge problem. I was trying to drink water through a straw from the plastic cup on my bedside stand.

The staff decided that the best way to give me the steroid pills and other meds was to crush them. I could then use water to wash them down. But every time I tried to drink, even with the pills crushed, I went into coughing spasms. I'd get them down, but it was quite an event each time.

Finally, around midnight, a male nurse came in and I attempted to swallow the medications he was giving me. I went into what had become normal coughing spasms. He had a fabulous suggestion that nobody else had thought of: lose the straw. He said, "By using the straw, you're flooding the back of your mouth, the vocal chords, and you're throwing too much, too fast at everything back there. Just take sips directly from the cup with your mouth, and you'll do much better." So, away the straw went—back to sipping I went, and he was right. I wish I knew his name so I could give him credit for the miraculous suggestion that eliminated many of the coughing spasms.

The only thing I could eat was liquid foods administered with very small spoonsful. Mostly, I had no appetite, so I "ate" a lot of soups. At one point I tried mashed potatoes, but that didn't work well; they clumped up and became too pasty inside my mouth. Several times I tried to move to a variety of different mushy foods without success. Each time I went into horrendous coughing and gagging spasms that completely exhausted me. Mushy foods would have to wait in favor of liquids. Onward and upward!

We were finding little baby solutions to problems that were constantly nagging me. Little did I know at the time that these little solutions would keep coming for the next three years. In fact, they continue to this day, and might for the rest of my life.

The first day or two after my surgery was pretty much like any other kind of surgery. The staff wanted to see if I could sit up on the side of my bed, or in a chair for a bit. Could I sit in the chair long enough to eat a meal? Since I was only eating liquids, it didn't take long and I was able to check that off their list.

On day two they wanted me to start walking with Don down the hallways even though there was concern I might fall. I suggested they give me a walker. Worked perfectly. I could now get up and go to the bathroom which meant no more bed pan, although I was told to ring the nurse so she could oversee my movements into and out of bed and bathroom. I did this a couple of times and then just did it all on my own.

Don and I were able to walk up the hallway, across the nurse's station, down the other hallway and back to the room a couple of times a day. Soon I could repeat that walk, always with Don, twice, and then three times before returning to the room. Seemed like a small feat but to us it was huge. Great improvement and great strides were being made.

Staying in the neurosurgery wing of a hospital is a little bit unnerving. There was one gentleman that wandered through the ward all day long. He would walk by my room, I don't know, maybe fifty times a day. Sometimes the staff could get him to lay down in his bed and rest. But mostly they let him wander, saying it was his thing. I don't know how long he'd been there, or how long he would be staying, but I found out that he'd had brain tumor surgery as well, and that was the effect it had on him. I never heard him talk. He looked coherent. He just wandered.

In the middle of my second night, a lady started screaming like someone was hurting her. At first I thought it was a nurse that had been attacked by another patient. I couldn't really make out any words, just screaming, but I did hear a man's voice yelling back at her. I reached for my phone debating whether to call 911.

The screaming continued for maybe fifteen or twenty minutes, then before I'd made a decision, calmed down. I found it all pretty frightening. One of the nurses came in my room the next day and told me that they had a new patient on the floor, and she was the screamer. They said this can happen post-op with certain types of brain tumor surgery. She proceeded to scream some more that day and the next night.

I kept thinking "Wow I'm really lucky that I can lay here and think rationally, talk rationally, and get up and walk around even if I need a walker." It made me feel really fortunate.

On my daily walker strolls I met an elderly gentleman that was also out with his wife using his walker. He seemed to be in the same condition as me. He was coherent, and Don and I would stop to talk with him. I was encouraged that other than re-learning walking and balance he was doing fine. He recovered nicely and went home a day or two before me. It was nice to know somebody else that had survived this and was doing fine, not wandering aimlessly or screaming their head off.

Email sent on 9/6/2009

Toni is going home today!

Toni is going home today and may do the updates herself. Toni and Don have requested no guests or phone calls for a week.

All your thoughts and prayers have been and continue to work!!

With love, Kim

(From Toni's email)

My team finally decided to release me on Sunday morning, 4 days post-surgery. It was quite the battle because they wanted me to go to a rehabilitation hospital. Don and I both said "No, no, no, I don't need to do that." Don was an orthopedic surgeon and we felt he was capable of watching over me at home. He had cancelled his work schedule so he could be with me twenty four hours a day. My mom had also moved close by, so she could come over and help if needed. We were clear with the staff, "I didn't need to be in a rehab hospital."

For whatever reason, the idea of being in a rehab center was really depressing to me. I felt like I'd prepared myself for this. I'd gotten myself mentally ready to go into the hospital, to have the surgery, and go home; not go into the hospital, have the surgery, and go to a different hospital. I just needed to be home and start recovering. If someone had forewarned me that after my stay on the neurosurgery floor they might transfer me to a rehab hospital, I might have prepared myself mentally, but this came at us out of the blue.

In fact, my previous family practitioner now ran the rehab hospital in Marin County that I would have been transferred to, so I would have known the director. But having the decision thrown at me was totally unacceptable, especially considering the progress I'd made so far and with the help I'd have at home.

Finally they agreed that if I could go into the hall and hang onto the railing, and walk back and forth, crisscrossing my feet quickly, they might acquiesce. I did everything they asked without falling. Actually, I did it really well. The rehabilitation guy said, "No you don't need to go to a rehab hospital; you can go ahead and go on home. You're steady enough, and you're walking with the walker; you'll do just fine."

Dr. Cheung came into my room before I left to check my hearing, which seemed to be improving. Dr. Parsa had initially said there would be a second surgery, but Dr. Cheung wasn't sure if a second surgery was necessary.

As the patient, I clung to that hope like a lifeline. One surgery was it; I was pretty sure I wasn't going to need a second. Dr. Cheung did say it was up to Dr. Parsa. That didn't matter to me. I crossed out the second surgery in my head and figured, "I am good to go."

I'd lost about fifty percent of the hearing in my right ear, but as Dr. Cheung had verified, it seemed to be slowly coming back. I still had double vision and a patch on one eye, so I looked like a pirate. I had no voice. I could only whisper. I had great difficulty swallowing food. But I was going home. That was the main thing for me. Brain tumor surgery on 9/2/2009 and going home 4 days later. Wow!

I remember Don driving me home from the hospital and it was a beautiful Sunday. All the sailboats were out on the bay and as we came across the Golden Gate Bridge. I looked to my right towards Alcatraz. That has always been such a stunning view. Ever since I moved to Marin in 1990, I'd get chills driving across the Golden Gate.

As we were driving across the bridge and I gazed at all the beauty around me with tears running down my cheeks, all I could do was try and whisper, "I wasn't sure I would ever see this again." The view was just so stunning, but all I could get out was a kind of hiccupping noise as I tried to form words.

I must have sounded really odd because Don said, "Oh my God, are you okay?" Here he was, trying to navigate traffic on the Golden Gate Bridge and thinking that I'm stroking out or something. "Yeah." I just kind of touched his arm, and nodded my head and said again, "Yes, I'm fine."

When I got control of myself a little more, I managed to tell him, "It's just such a gorgeous sight and I didn't know if I would ever see it again." We didn't know when I went into surgery, if I might come out deaf, blind, or physically or mentally disabled. The whole process had been one big step into the unknown.

Don has since told me that I am just a miracle to him. He's said that with everything they did during the surgery, lifting up my brain and moving things around, that there was no way I should be anything but a vegetable.

So, home I went on a Sunday morning; just in time for the opening of the NFL season. I got home probably about halfway through the 49er's game. They played

Arizona, at Arizona, and won 20-16. Life was good!

I sat on the couch and watched my Niners win, eating one piece of popcorn at a time. I figured it might be a good way to start training my body to accept solid food. Since I'm kind of a popcorn addict, Don just laughed at my training method, but who knows, maybe it did help.

I was back with my dogs, my husband, my house, my peace of mind, and peacefulness at night. I didn't have people screaming, running up and down the halls, and alerts going out over the loud speaker system. Hospitals weren't really made for sleeping, and I was looking forward to catching up. Unfortunately the doctors sent me home on steroids. I'd been on them ever since my surgery to relieve the swelling on my brain stem. The steroids made it really, really hard to sleep.

Home turned out to be a little less exciting than I'd thought, simply because I couldn't really do anything except lay around and recover. I didn't want to sleep during the day because, thanks to the steroids, I was already having trouble sleeping at night. I had spent too many nights in the hospital watching the minute hand tick by. The non-sleep pattern was getting old fast.

I watched a lot of movies, watched a lot of TV, played a lot of solitaire on the computer, and started to get a little down and depressed. My son kept saying, "Just go outside and sit; it's a beautiful fall day." It was now mid-September. He said, "I know you. You're not a good rester. You're too active. Get out in the back yard and do something."

It was a little spooky for me to just go and sit outside because I still had no feeling on the right side of my head. If a bird had landed on my head, I wouldn't have known it. I could be bitten. I could be stung. And I wouldn't have felt a thing. I didn't feel comfortable just sitting out back in a chair with nobody out there to watch over me except the dogs.

I stayed in the house. I did keep doing the guided imagery. I had a guided imagery for healing after surgery. I kept focusing on that, kept focusing on my recovery, and kept focusing on having positive people around me; people praying all over the world; uplifting people.

During this time I learned an important lesson from a friend of Don's, Sara. She worked with him in Sacramento. I'm not sure I'd ever met Sara, maybe once, but during my entire recovery process, through both surgeries, I got a get-well card from her once a week for probably two months, maybe three.

My friends and family send get-well cards when a friend or family member is sick. We go to the store, pick out a card, and send it. But to get one from someone I hadn't met was so nice and so thoughtful, that I've adopted her policy. Her policy of sending a card out weekly until the person is completely mended.

People don't recover from surgery in a day, or a week, or even a month. And during

the recovery period they need positive
stuff coming at them all the time. It's all
too easy in our busy society and lives, to
send off a card, scratch it from our To Do
list, and move on to the next item. I kept
all her cards. I kept all the other cards I
got during that time period too. I wanted
to remember the people who took the time to
think of me, that took the time to do that
once a week. Get a card. Get a stamp. Do
everything required to send it out. Really
impressive. I hope to be able to do that
for other people now and pass that
wonderfulness along.

Chapter 6 It Must Be Toni Because I Can't Hear Her

"Oh, my friend, it's not what they take away from you that counts. It's what you do with what you have left." —Hubert Humphrey

Jasen came in, my second or third day home, and proceeded to be our chef. He is a wonderful cook and made us a bunch of good meals that we could package into the freezer in two-person servings, so I would have some really nutritious stuff going into me every day.

Jasen commented to me later, not at that time, that his initial thought when he saw me was, "Where's my mom? What have they done with her?"

I thought I looked pretty good but I'm sure that was relative. Apparently to fresh eyes I looked like I was struggling.

Throughout my twenties and thirties and well into my forties, I had been on a women's soccer team, playing competitively. Playing competitive tennis. I think for Jasen to see his mother with a walker was shocking, and he just didn't know how to process that.

I'm glad he didn't say anything at the time. He didn't tell me anything until probably a year later when I could handle hearing it. I would not have wanted to hear it the first time I saw him.

A few days after settling in at home, I called our family that had grandchildren. I wanted the kids to hear my voice, and know that I made it and I was doing fine. Their parents were really glad I made that effort; they had explained to their kids what had happened to Grandma, and even though my voice was still weak, the kids could still hear me.

I would call my dad maybe once a week, down in South Texas. When my stepmother answered, and I said, "Hello, hello" in a whisper, Jane would answer, "Hello, who's there? Hello?" It got to where she would turn to my dad and say, "Robert I think it must be Toni because I can't hear anything." Then he would get on the phone and I would whisper loud enough so he could hear and know that I was okay.

If I only uttered a word or two, he could usually make out what I said. When I tried to say whole sentences, it came out too garbled for him. I learned to get my thoughts out in whispering short bursts.

My dad had not been able to make it for my surgery because my stepmother was so ill; he needed to take care of her. I think it was really hard for him not to be in on the day-to-day loop of what was going on with me. He did tell me later to thank Don for contacting him so frequently. Many other people were also grateful because Don had kept them so well informed. I heard repeatedly how great a job he did keeping everyone updated.

Friends heard via e-mail that I was okay, especially right after the surgery, so they knew not to worry.

About a week after coming home, I had a follow up appointment with Dr. Parsa. He set my second surgery for October 28, 2009, which really slammed me against the wall. I had somehow convinced myself that I wouldn't have to prepare for a second surgery; that this ordeal was now done and we could all move on.

Dr. Parsa had de-bulked the tumor back where it was pressing against my brain stem and brain. He had gone in at the base of the skull and relieved a lot of pressure by taking out the bulk of the tumor, but he still needed to go in from the top of my head and get to it where it threatened my optic nerve and the auditory nerve near a carotid artery; some really ugly places.

He had warned us after the first surgery, that there was no way he could get out all the tumor because it was wrapped too tightly around too many things, and if he got too close he could leave me deaf; blind and/or physically or mentally impaired.

Because it was such a slow growing tumor, Dr. Parsa estimated that it had been there twenty to thirty years. He felt that if he just de-bulked the remainder, I would live a normal life span. Whatever portion

he was unable to remove would grow so
slowly that I would probably never know it
was there.

Now that my next surgery was
scheduled, my biggest dread was the thought
of going back into the hospital. I wasn't
worried about the surgery itself, because I
had complete faith in Dr. Parsa and his
remarkable skills. But I dreaded being in
the hospital for another five-to-seven days
with all the craziness of the neurosurgery
unit and the patients in it.

I went back to working with guided
imagery, and relying on my support group of
family and friends, staying around positive
and upbeat people.

Don didn't want me out and about very
much, because we were coming into the fall
flu and cold season. He did agree to drop
me at a coffee shop on really, really nice
days. I would sit outside with my mom and
George (my step-father), or Don's daughter
Elizabeth. Elizabeth was back on the boat
for this second surgery. She now understood
not to say how terrible and awful this was.

I set an example for her that this might be a challenge, but one step at a time, you make your way through the challenge.

As long as I stayed outside and they went in and got the coffee or tea, keeping me out of the reach of coughing and sneezing people, then the coffee shop scene was fine by Don.

My Mom and George found a small bakery in Novato, with a light midmorning crowd, so we went there maybe once a week to have tea, chat, and get caught up. It was nice to get out of the house. And it was so nice to have them living just a couple of miles from me.

I'm not a big stay-at-home person. I need to get out at least once a day and do things, be around people. I get my energy from being around others and seeing life move around me.

Initially, after the first surgery, I would meet my mom at Don's church. When Don went to mass, my mom and I would walk around the local neighborhood for forty five minutes, before returning home with

Don. I found out that these almost solitary walks did nothing for me, other than give me a little exercise. I really needed to be around people, and walking up and down neighborhood streets not interacting with anybody or doing anything in particular, gave me no mental lift at all.

What I really needed was to be in downtown Novato, walking around in traffic and seeing people and cars and hearing honking and whatever, to really keeping me going and trucking along.

Chapter 7 Cases of Cough Drops

The coughing continued to get worse. Whenever I tried to eat I would cough and cough until I gagged, completely out of breath, gasping for air. It seemed my body, and I assume all bodies, have a built in mechanism for this. Just when I was completely out of air and about to drop to my knees, my body would freeze for a split second and I would sneeze. The first time this happened it seemed completely bizarre to me. But it filled my lungs with air and the coughing stopped, until the next time. I found it completely amazing that we have a built-in mechanism that senses, "Okay we're in danger here. We don't have air. Let's do a sneeze." When we sneeze, it fills our lungs with air and once again we're good to go.

At night the coughing was also bad, even though I wasn't eating anything. After surgery, I always had a tickle in my throat. I would wake up and cough, cough,

cough, until I had no air left. Then I'd sneeze and eventually fall back asleep.

Because it was hard to sleep due to the steroids, it was worse to wake up coughing, so I tried cough drops and they actually seemed to help. I expect what they were doing was helping me create more moisture in my throat so that as I swallowed my throat wasn't drying out, which seemed to be causing the tickle. I got so I would fall asleep every night with a cough drop in my mouth.

To save time and money, I went to Amazon.com to see if I could order cough drops by the case. I could and did. I would have an unlimited supply at this point. I kept taking them and taking them. I think they ended up being really hard on my stomach, and most likely caused some problems down the road.

To keep from having coughing fits in public, I traveled with them during the day, in my pocket, around the house, to the coffee shop, wherever I might be going.

When I went back for another MRI, I took cough drops with me. I explained to the tech that I was going to take a cough drop before I went in, and laid several more on the counter in case I needed one during the MRI. They could pull me out, give me a cough drop, and start me all over again if necessary.

Luckily, I never needed them to do that; the one cough drop lasted long enough that I could get through the procedure.

It wasn't until 2012, that I figured out how to control the coughing. In talking with Dr. Rossman one day, I mentioned that I never coughed when we ate out in a restaurant. He wondered why, since at most every meal at home during 2009 and 2010 I would start each meal with coughing spasms.

What I figured out was that at a restaurant the first thing they give you is a glass of water. Right away I'd pick up the water and sip away. Basically, what I was doing was priming the pump. I was getting my esophagus ready to accept drink, food, whatever.

Of course no waiter brought me a glass of water when I was at home. I'd cook all of our meals, set them on the table and we'd eat.

Finally, three years later, I have learned to drink several sips of water before I eat and it's helped a ton.

Another problem that presented itself after I returned home from the hospital was how to get food to our house? I wasn't driving so I couldn't just run over to the store. Don had never done the grocery shopping. I would have had to be very specific about what I wanted him to get: brand name, container size, and also description of where it was at the grocery store. I used to wonder why anyone would have their groceries delivered. You had to pay for this service. I guess I assumed those people must be super busy and couldn't take the time to go to the store. Why was there a Safeway.com? Well, I found out.

With groceries delivered to my house, I could get what I wanted, when I wanted it, without going into long explanations for Don to figure out. We did a lot of Safeway.com, and it kept me well stocked with cough drops as well as the liquids it was necessary for me to be on until I could move to solid food.

Don was like the Energizer Bunny at this point. When I wanted to take my daily shower he would get the water at the right temperature, put the walker in the shower (physically into the shower) so I'd have something to hold on to, then he'd hang out until I was done. At that point he would help me out of the shower, get the walker out of the shower, dry it off, and we were good to go again.

He didn't want me getting up in the middle of the night to use the bathroom without help for fear I'd fall down. My instructions were to wake him up. That just seems amazing to me now, because I'd wake him up at least twice a night, maybe three times, and he'd get up, make sure I got the walker okay, got into the bathroom okay, and got back to bed okay. I think he must have been completely exhausted by the time

I was able to start doing stuff on my own, but he never complained, never said anything, and just kept doing what needed to be done to make sure I was safe. How can I ever express enough gratitude for this kind of caring?!?

The one thing Don kept pounding into my head was, "You cannot fall. DO NOT fall. Whatever you do, don't take any risks. Don't fall." Through the whole process, I never did fall. He was concerned about me hitting my head, or jarring anything inside my brain.

Additionally, in order to get to the tumor during the first surgery, the surgeon had to take out a piece of bone in the back of my skull, do the surgery, put the bone back, and then insert a piece of titanium screen to hold everything in place.

We were told that the bone grows back where it was before, but we never knew at what point that bone was completely reattached. Maybe it's still loose. Bottom line, we sure as heck didn't want me bumping it, knocking it, or damaging it in

any way so I'd have to go back in and have
more surgery to repair it. It was really,
really impressed on me: DO NOT FALL.

There were a couple of meals that I
couldn't wait to have once I got home from
the hospital. One was a Caesar salad with
grilled shrimp from California Grill in
Novato, CA. Sadly, I found out that
lettuce, once it got into my mouth, just
kind of melts and gets all soggy. I didn't
have the ability to swallow it past my
vocal chords. I could only cough and gag my
way through the salad.

We didn't learn until the second
surgery, how bad off my vocal chords were.
Don asked the anesthesiologist to look
before he tubed me, and he reported that,
"Yes, the vocal chords are partially
paralyzed."

What happened was, during the surgery
the muscles on the right side of my face,
and partially in other places in my body,
had clamped down. The muscles basically
said, "Hey, we don't like what's going on
here, so we're all going to band together,

really tightly, and try and protect everything we can."

As a result, when I smiled my lower jaw veered off to the right. Most of the right side of my skull and face were numb because nerves had been severed during the surgery. My jaw did not line up at all. To complicate matters, my lower jaw was also pulled back somewhat because the mastoid muscle had clamped down and wouldn't let go. I wasn't able to adjust my jaw back to its normal chewing position, so I had to chew as best I could without my teeth lining up. A food like lettuce that just melted and turned wimpy, was impossible to manipulate in my mouth. Because my vocal chords were partially paralyzed, they didn't vibrate much, so once I started coughing it was hard to cough away the irritant, whether a small crumb or a piece of wimpy lettuce.

The other meal that I really, really wanted was a pasta meal from Marin Joe's. I was thrilled one day when my two stepdaughters brought that over and stayed for lunch with us.

I must have looked really bizarre trying to eat it, but they were kind enough not to say anything. For starters, I couldn't cut the pasta off the spoon with my teeth because they didn't line up. The pasta hung from my mouth, wobbled all over the place, bumped me in the chin, bumped onto my shirt. I was a complete mess, and so frustrated as I really, really wanted to eat that meal.

After about a year of eating with my jaw still misaligned, I learned to cut foods by putting them against my lower lip and biting down gently. Eating pasta that way worked great because it was a soft food. Anything much firmer and I risked cutting my lip.

As a result I decided to stick with liquids or really mushy foods.

One unexpected benefit of my difficulties in eating was that I'd lost twenty pounds. That wasn't a bad thing. I'd been trying to lose weight for quite some time, so it appeared I was now on the brain tumor diet and it was working really well.

Twenty pounds down, a few more to go, and I'd be happy with my weight.

Slowly, I learned how to get my tongue involved in the eating process, although the right side of my face/mouth was still numb. It was as if somebody had drawn a line down the center of my tongue, from front to back, and half of it was numb and tingly, and the other half just fine. Sometimes I would bite down on my right cheek by mistake, and while I never felt the pain, I knew by the taste of blood that I'd screwed up.

With practice, I did manage to manipulate my tongue so I could take slightly mushy food, like a cooked apple, and crush it against my palate. That I could swallow.

I joked during that time about flossing in the dark. Since my right side was numb, I couldn't feel my teeth or gums. Hopefully, at some point, it would all come back, and I would know if flossing in the dark was working.

Going to the dentist was often problematic. I had no way to know if I was in danger of having tooth decay or gum disease in the right side of my mouth because I couldn't feel pain there. Nine times out of ten, when I opened by mouth wide at the dentist, I'd go into coughing spasms.

Luckily my dentist was really patient with me. I'd book an appointment to have my teeth cleaned and checked, but if it turned out to be a bad day for opening my mouth wide, I'd cancel. Finally I just toughed it out and hoped I could get through the appointment. I explained to the hygienist what was happening, and told her not to worry if I went into a coughing spasm, it would be over soon.

I couldn't drive yet, not with double vision and a patch over my right eye. Although I felt like I could have managed, it seemed wise not to attempt it at that time.

Intellectually my brain seemed fine. I was functioning at my normal level. My vocabulary was fine, as was my thinking process, and none of us were noticing any mental gaps. So I probably could have driven, because in a sitting position, my balance was fine.

With vision in one eye only, you have no depth perception. Depth perception is created by viewing things out of two eyes. It wasn't something I ever thought about but now that I had monocular vision, it was certainly something I had to deal with. If someone tosses you a ball, your vision signals your brain how fast the ball is coming at you and at what angle. With monocular vision, you get none of those cues. I am constantly reaching out for something, change from the clerk, a thread in my weaving, and yet I grab thin air. I'm just unable to see how far away things are from me. I've even poured water all over the restaurant table when I was sure I was pouring it into my glass.

Over time, you learn to touch the side of your glass with the water container and then pour. You create your own workable solutions. But most amazing is how the brain adjusts to monocular vision. I can catch a ball now when it is tossed to me. I reach slowly for a thread and my brain guides my hand to it. My brain reads light and shadows as I walk down the street. When I step off the curb, I now know roughly how far my foot needs to go to reach the street. Amazing how my brain has compensated for the loss of one eye.

It was only when trying to walk that my balance was off. My right inner ear had been damaged, which threw off my balance. I would have loved the freedom to conduct my life in my normal way, including driving, but it didn't seem to be an option at this time.

Chapter 8 This is My Normal?

I remember sitting at my computer one day, telling my husband, "I just want my life to get back to normal." And he said, "This is normal."

I understood what he was saying, that this is my new normal, but I completely rejected that. I had no intention of being like this--trapped in my house and using a walker for the rest of my life. I would recover, and I would be able to conduct my affairs as I had before. I'd be able to weave on my looms. I'd be able to do everything except maybe play soccer or tennis. That was fine. I hadn't played those sports in years.

There might be a few limitations, but I had a lot of the world still to see and I planned on seeing it, flying to whatever destination I wished, walking all over, and taking it all in. This may have been my temporary new normal, but it sure as hell wasn't going to be my permanent new normal.

Chapter 9 Second Surgery

My second surgery was scheduled for October 28, 2009. About two weeks before the surgery, I was down to using a cane, not the walker, and my double vision just went away. I'd been wearing an eye patch when I was around the house, or at the coffee shop, or walking around or out with the dogs.

When I went to bed each night, I would look up at the top of my bookshelf where I kept a picture of my father and stepmother. Without the eye patch I saw two pictures of them because of my double vision.

But one night I saw only one image of the picture. Nobody could explain how this happened, because double vision doesn't just go away within a matter of hours without some training. The best guess was that my brain realized, "Okay, this isn't right. I'm going to cancel out this second image." The brain has the ability to do this—for instance when people wear contact lenses for astigmatism, but no one expected it to happen to me.

I went into the second surgery with no more double vision and came out with double vision and a right eyelid that no longer lifted. In a sense the double vision was no longer an issue because I had monocular vision instead.

If I lifted the lid of my right eye the double vision returned. If I tried to walk with the right eyelid lifted, I started stumbling. I couldn't see where I was going because everything was askew. One eye looked one way and one eye looked the other. Wearing the eye patch was a pain in the neck. Nobody seems to have designed a comfortable eye patch. The one they gave me at the hospital was cardboard, of all things. It didn't mold around my eye, and it didn't sit well on my cheek. It would move around a lot and end up off.

I tried another one that had some foamy stuff around the edges that at least held it up, like it was hovering over my eye. That was a small improvement as it wasn't actually sitting on my eyelid the way the cardboard one did. But I've never found a comfortable patch.

For the second surgery, the surgical team went in from the top of my skull. What Dr. Parsa told me he was going to do was make an incision and peel my skull back. At that point I said "Enough. I'm on a need-to-know basis, and I don't need to know that." It sounded very gross and super painful. Dr. Parsa did say that after surgery I would have my head wrapped in a turban. Cool! I'd travelled to Turkey nine times, so I was excited to be a "Sultaness." I figured I'd take a picture to send to my friends in Turkey. You have to create and hold onto every bit of humor you can generate with events like this. It's all about attitude, attitude, attitude.

But, alas, no turban. The upper part of my head was wrapped in gauze and they placed a small gauze cap over that. Maybe the docs didn't know what a turban looked like. This was not even close. Bummer!

Again the surgeons needed to de-bulk, or thin out, the tumor. In this surgery he would cut close to the pituitary gland, the optic nerve, the auditory nerve, and a lot of other nerves in that area. The best he could do was get as close as possible since the tumor was wrapped around those nerves, and again, he would not be able to get it all out, just most of it. My surgeons, since this was a super slow-growing tumor, after this surgery I should have a normal life expectancy, and hopefully, no other complications.

This was the plan: another ten-hour surgery, another four or five days in the hospital, and then recuperation and recovery at home after my hospital stay.

Email sent out 10/28/2009

Toni is out of surgery! Hi Everyone, Toni just got out of surgery a little bit ago. Surgery went "really, really well" and took half the time they expected. However she will need radiation therapy follow up.

Last recovery was a long and hard road, but all your prayers and thoughts were very appreciated!

Kim

- From Toni's email, doing group updates until Toni kicks me off again :)

Email sent out on 10/29/2009

Toni good update. Early Bird update: Just found out that after Toni woke from surgery last night, around dinner time, she had all her faculties intact. She could move everything, whisper, hear and see... all nerve related functions which didn't come easily last surgery.

A few have asked "Why radiation therapy?" I just got told the surgeon couldn't remove tiny parts of the tumor, so the radiation therapy is being used to zap out remaining tiny pieces of tumor... "Sweeping up the dust."

All your love is being passed on to Toni and Don.

Kim

At this point, the NFL season had progressed and I had access to most of the games in the hospital, so I wasn't in a big rush to get back home. The opening weekend of the season is always so exciting after waiting all spring and summer for NFL football to return. Now the season was in full swing and I'd just catch it from my hospital bed.

Going into the hospital, after being there before, I would have gladly fled after the first day. It's just again, crazy things happening on that ward: people screaming, a lot of moaning.

I can't explain why I had no pain after this surgery. Don reminded me that I did have pain the first day after the first surgery. I apparently have no recollection of this as I may have been too under the anesthesia. I'll stick with saying I had no pain, as I don't recall any maybe because the surgeons had cut so many nerves in the skull. Not sure.

What Dr. Parsa was going to do sounded really painful. I know he was cutting nerves when he cut through my scalp. As a result, I experienced fuzziness in my nerve endings on the right side of my head as they reconnected, but not pain. The fuzziness made it difficult to get to sleep. No matter what position I laid in, it was like little pin pricks shooting off randomly all over the right side of my face, and just my face, not my head.

I avoided all the pain medication. Staff would come in with a pain pill to ask if I needed it. I asked if it would help me sleep and they said no, the pill would probably make it harder to sleep. During all my nights in the hospital, I would watch the minutes and hours tick off on the clock at the foot of my bed. I couldn't sleep and there was nothing else to do.

At one point, I tried the TV, but the limited hearing in my right ear made it noisy and annoying. I couldn't seem to concentrate on it at all.

There was one area of pain that
perplexed me, and continued to do so for
three years post-surgery. I had pain in my
hip area. On my first follow up appointment
with Dr. Parsa, I was given a copy of the
human body and ask to circle anywhere I had
pain. I circled only the hip area and wrote
a brief note about it.

Both Dr. Parsa and Don said that this
pain could not have come from the surgery.
In hind sight, I think none of us
communicated clearly. It wasn't until three
years later, when I discovered Shiatsu
Massage, that I figured it out. I explained
to the massage therapist that I had hip
pain and perhaps they could help. I said I
went into surgery with no hip pain, but
from the moment I left intensive care and
was put into a room, I could feel intense
hip pain. The pain made it difficult to
sleep and caused it to hurt when I went up
and down steps. It was even painful to step
off the curb of the sidewalk.

The massage therapist's comment was
simple, "If I had lain in one position for

10 hours of surgery, I'd have hip pain too."

Wow. Of course. From the surgery itself, nothing Dr. Parsa did to my head or my brain caused it. It came from body positioning. And certainly during brain surgery, they can't be moving or rotating my body to avoid that level of stiffness.

Shiatsu Massage did reach the pain and eliminated it after about four months of twice-monthly treatments. Aki, at the Shiatsu Center in Portland Oregon, did tremendous body work on me, loosening muscles that had been rigid for three years.

After three days in the hospital following the second surgery, it was nice to be home again; nice to come into my own house with my dog watchers, my mom and ~~my~~ stepfather there to greet me.

Apparently I had a black eye. It looked worse, according to my mom, than the one Frank Gore received the previous Sunday during the 49ers game.

Email sent out on 10/30/2009

Toni's update…."Continuing fast recovery: no pain, no walker, home this weekend."

Toni sounded herself on a strong-whisper voicemail she left last night making sure I didn't miss a work-related issue she identified... best phone call I've received in a long time! —Kim

My hospital stay was less eventful this time; at least when they got me into a room, they knew I was there from the minute I arrived.

Also, I didn't experience as much vomiting after the surgery. Since the staff knew going in that it had happened the first time, they put a bunch of anti-nausea drugs in the I.V. Thankfully, I didn't have to go through all that again.

I did have to have, within the first 24 hours, another MRI. Since I couldn't really swallow well, and I was not breathing out of my right nostril at all, going into an MRI and lying down on my back trying to swallow and breathe at the same time was just challenging.

I had my cough drops with me, but at times I was concerned about clearing my throat. I was afraid I would go into a coughing spasm while in the MRI, so instead, I let saliva dribble out of my mouth and down my neck.

These after-surgery MRI's, because they involve a contrast dye, take at least half an hour, sometimes up to an hour. That is a long time to be lying there not breathing well; concerned I was going to go into a coughing spasm. I tried to take my mind away from it all and be somewhere else. I talked to my dad in my head. Each time I was rolled into the machine, I imagined my dad saying to me, "Okay, Toni, here we go again, you're going to make it. You're tough, just gut this out, and just keep talking to me." So I make up conversations with my dad while I was lying in the machine. That helped a lot and kept me distracted from where I was at the moment.

The MRI machine itself, made a series of bump-bump-bump, thump-thump-thump noises, so I turned the beating into a song and tried to sing along in my head. Doing that helped me concentrate on something else besides the fact that I was trapped in the machine, making super sure I didn't move, and didn't touch the side. God forbid I should do anything but lay frozen in time until they were done.

The MRI results pleased the staff, now it was up to me. No more surgeries, let's just get on with it and recover. Get back to my kind of normal; not the kind of normal I was experiencing at this point.

Email sent out on 10/30/2009

I'm home. Got out of the hospital today around 2. So very nice to be home.

They say I breezed thru this one. Didn't feel like that to me. But I guess I came out of this one even better than the last one.

Thanks for everyone's help, prayers, and kind thoughts. Couldn't have done it without you. This was definitely a group

surgery. No more are planned. They
wanted to do two and that's been
done now. That's enough already.

Does look like radiation is in my
future when they determine it is
the time to start it. We don't
know when that will be, nor do
they. It will be determined on how
the tumor reacts to all this
surgery.—T

Chapter 10 Pins and Needles

After my first surgery and again after my second, the doctors gave me permission to continue acupuncture. There's no definitive way to tell if this was actually helping me or not, but it kept my mood lifted and the clinic was a nice, quiet place for me to go and interact with the people.

Don drove me to the acupuncture clinic and waited for me while I received treatment, then drove me back home. My acupuncturist, Dr. Rossman, was a joy to be around, as was his staff. All of them were very encouraging and positive.

One day, after my second surgery, I got a text from Kim, my step-daughter: "Look outside your front door."

I opened the door and there sat the sweetest heart plate. It was a ceramic plate that our granddaughter Charlie had hand painted a heart onto. What a thoughtful thing to do. That plate still holds a special place in my heart.

Chapter 11 Grace?

"No One Ever Said Life is fair. Just Eventful." —Carol Burnett

One day after my second surgery, I went in for an acupuncture treatment and Dr. Rossman's comment to me was, "Toni, I have to tell you, you've handled all of this with such grace."

Grace?

Grace was not something I ever thought I had. I could kick a soccer ball, hit a baseball, and had been a tomboy all my life. I loved it. But grace? That didn't seem like something a tomboy had, or could ever have. It brought a chuckle, but it also brought back a memory of a Seinfeld episode.

Elaine is working as an executive assistant for this guy in New York City, and he admits that he knew Jackie Onassis. The one thing that so impressed him about Jackie O was the 'grace' she had. Elaine became obsessed with grace. What is grace? How do you get grace? How do you keep grace? Where is this thing called grace? To be told that I had grace (chuckling) was just amazing to me. If Jackie O had grace, how could I have it also?

I went home, sent my mom an e-mail, and told her, "My name is no longer Toni, it's now Grace. Just call me Grace." For a while, I was known as Grace. I was delighted that I had grace, that somehow I had found it. I had no intention of letting it go. What a thing to find on my brain tumor journey.

In thinking about it, I understood what Dr. Rossman meant. Throughout this journey I hadn't freaked out; I didn't run around going "Oh my God," or "Why me?" I didn't indulge in pity parties. This journey did make me wonder, "Who is Toni? Who am I now that I've had a brain tumor?" I didn't want to be defined by my brain tumor. I didn't want to be, "I've had a brain tumor Toni." I wanted to be, "Toni who once upon a time had a brain tumor." I didn't want to run around with a badge of courage on my chest, "Look at me, I survived a brain tumor." Well-meaning friends or family would tell me how brave I had been. That seemed an odd word to me for what I had been through. To me people who were brave chose a path that might put them in danger but moved forward, into the danger anyway. This was not a path I chose. It wasn't a risky behavior in my life that produced this brain tumor. I simply had it and then had to figure out what to do with it. That didn't constitute bravery to me.

Every once in a while, it would flip through my mind "Who am I now?" It clearly does change you. Something that dramatic in your life does change you.

About that same time, a good friend of mine, Richard, had his own health issue. We're both rug weavers. I had met him at a weaving class in Mendocino, years before and we'd become good friends. Word came to me from someone that Richard had had bypass surgery, so I was keeping in touch with him a little bit more than normal.

He had told me a month or so earlier that he had a blocked artery, and the doctors wanted to do bypass surgery. He'd

been an alternative medicine practitioner
for years, so he wanted to fix it with
alternative medicine.

There are places in our lives for
alternative medicine and there are places
for traditional medicine. Those lines are a
little more clearly drawn for me now that
I've had these two surgeries and then
turned to alternative medicine to clean up
the effects of the surgeries on my body.

It was worrisome to me that Richard
felt he could fix this "mentally" and make
it go away. I'm a huge believer in what we
can accomplish mentally, through guided
imagery and visualization, but a blocked
artery was a clear case designed for
traditional medicine.

Richard collapsed one night waiting in
line at a restaurant. Standing behind him
in line was his cardiologist. Richard was
rushed to the hospital and the bypass was
performed.

I received this e-mail from Richard
about the same time I was thinking "Who am
I now?" In it he said:

"Toni, I don't know who I am now."
I find it kind of depressing and I
don't even know why I'm thinking
this, but I don't know who Richard
is."

It hit me like a brick. I hadn't
really put into words that I was thinking
the same thing about myself.

When I read the email, I thought, "Oh
my God, I can completely relate to the 'Who
am I?' question." "Who am I?" We e-mailed
back and forth, and I wrote:

"Pretty much we're the same people
we were before; we've just been
given another shot at life, so
let's use it to the maximum, and
remember to do that as much as we
can every day for as long as we're
alive. And we have each other to
reinforce that."

I would e-mail him quite often,
because I know that when there's some sort
of surgery to the heart, or a heart attack,
it messes big time with endorphins. A
person can get very depressed. After my
first heart attack in 1986 (I had a second
one in 2001), I became suicidal. I was

concerned this could happen to Richard. I wish doctors would tell people. I'm told doctors don't tell people because if they did, it might lead to depression. I just think that's silly. Everyone I've known who has gone through a heart issue, has ended up depressed, completely perplexed by it, and wondering what the heck is wrong with them.

If doctors would just inform them, "Hey this might happen to you; be on the lookout for it. Tell your relatives to be on the lookout so they can help you get through it," rather than ignore the potential, then people recovering from heart issues might have stronger coping mechanisms during recovery.

Richard and I decided through our email exchanges that we were still the same people as before, with a little more wisdom and grace. That was a nice way to look at it.

I was released from the hospital after the second surgery on October 30th, 2009. For Thanksgiving that year I wanted to cook a full Thanksgiving meal. I wanted to see if I was capable of that, not physically but mentally. Could I remember the dishes we usually had? Could I make them? Could I have them done all at the same time? A large meal like that takes a lot of coordination and timing. My mom was worried about me taking it on, but I needed to see if I could do it. I could. The meal was a success.

As we sat down to eat, I was thrilled to know that I'd gotten my brain to organize such a huge effort. I shopped using Safeway.com. My mom made the dressing and cornbread, but everything else, the turkey, gravy, mashed potatoes, sweet potatoes, scalloped corn—all of it, I did myself. And got it all ready and done at the same time.

As a result, I now felt my brain function was normal, even if we hadn't tested it beyond a few normal conversations around the house.

We had cancelled all of the art festivals we were to participate in during

the fall of 2009. In the spring of 2009 I
had listed many of my hand woven scarves
for sale at Amazon.com. Now, in the fall of
2009, I was selling scarves like crazy
through Amazon and barely able to keep up.
I kept selling the same ones over and over,
so I'd have to remake them, remake them,
and remake them. Certain scarves were just
very popular.

I had learned from my first surgery to
get my loom ready before I went in so that
when I came home I was ready to weave. It
was comforting to discover that once I came
home, I could weave and create patterns
just fine.

After my first surgery, while still
using my walker, I could take my walker and
walk over, kind of lift myself up onto the
weaving bench and weave. I could do it all
on my own. No one helping, no one else
creating the designs for me, no one lifting
me onto the bench. I was getting closer to
my 'normal'.

Chapter 12 Driving Force

Email sent on 1/2/2010

Happy New Year to All

Hope all had a great holiday season.

 Just wanted to give a brief update. Have started driving so now have much of my freedom back. I walk 1-2 miles per day and am doing great.

Just yesterday I put on my headset to listen to an audiobook as I walked and put the ear plug in the right ear....Wow! I could hear. I could hear out of my right ear almost as well as my left ear. Yahoo! So hearing still seems to be continuing to improve.

Still waiting for the right eye lid to open but they say any day. Meeting with the radiologist on Jan. 12 to determine if he wants to do radiation to shave off tiny bits of tumor that were in dangerous places. He may want to watch and wait to see if the blood supply has been cut to those pieces of tumor and they die on their own. Jan. 12 is a consult

with him. He'll lay out his plan
for I guess gamma knife radiation
at that time.

Happy New Year!—T

I had been relying on everybody else
to drive me around from September 1, 2009
to now; my mom, my husband, my son,
Elizabeth, my step-daughter. Someone picked
me up and drove me wherever I needed to go,
stayed with me or walked with me, and then
dropped me back home. Thank God they were
all able to do that. Everyone was gracious,
helpful and eager to do whatever they
could.

But I needed my freedom back. I needed
to be able to go out, put the key in the
ignition when I wanted to, drive away when
I wanted to, and come back when I wanted
to. I needed that boost of freedom to get
back to where I once had been, and find my
normal. And now here I was, on January 2,
2010, back to driving again.

There were of course concerns about me
driving with just one eye. Then I
remembered that my first mother-in-law,

Elayne, had an eye damaged in childhood. She had never driven with eyesight in both eyes. From the day she started driving, she was a one-eyed driver. I talked to her about it and I realized that other people we knew also had one eye and drove just fine. It wasn't something people couldn't overcome. It was just a matter of safety.

We decided the way to start out was to first let me try driving around a parking lot. We went out to Costco in Novato, late in the day when there wasn't much traffic. I drove around an empty part of the parking lot to make sure my balance wasn't an issue. It turned out that balance wasn't an issue at all as long as I was sitting down. We decided the next step was to have Don go with me everywhere I went for perhaps a week, to make sure I was doing okay.

We both knew there wasn't really much he could do if I suddenly veered into oncoming traffic; he could grab the wheel and whip the car back, but if I was unable to stop, or didn't push the brake in time, there wasn't anything he could do from the passenger's side, except maybe scream or wiggle my arm, to keep us out of an accident. We avoided the freeway for the first week to test how I handled driving around town.

Again, I did just fine. After a week, Don said he felt comfortable with me driving by myself. But neither of us wanted me on the freeway yet. We weren't sure how I would react to faster traffic. Would I be able to tell that it was moving faster?

In all my steps back to my "normal," I never wanted to do anything that left my loved ones worrying about me. We all needed to be on the same page so that when I left the house on my own, everyone felt comfortable.

Because it's really hard to get away from work when you work out of your home—there are no sick days and no coffee breaks—you tend to just sit there and work and work and work, and then suddenly realize "Oh my gosh, it's lunchtime, I better eat something." So you have lunch. "Oh my gosh, it's dinnertime, I better eat something." You tend to just work around the clock. This was nothing new; I'd been working sixteen hour days for years.

My dad suggested I take a coffee break every day. He said, "Just get out, take the newspaper with you, go sit in a coffee shop, have a cup of coffee, and read the paper. Just clear your head, you'll be much more productive, and not such a workaholic."

We moved to Novato in 1996, and any day that I was in town, I was at Peet's in Novato, having a cup of coffee, and reading my Wall Street Journal.

There was a manager there named John, who always knew what I ordered every day. After my surgery, when I came in with my cane, or first my walker, he just started getting it for me.

One day I went to Peet's needing to buy some loose tea for home. The tables were situated so that a particular table, occupied by a chatting couple, blocked the view of the case where the tea was displayed. They didn't notice that I was trying to look over their shoulders at the tea.

I wasn't aware of what was going on in the rest of the coffee shop; didn't know if it was busy, not busy. I hadn't paid attention to who was working that day. I just knew I needed tea. I was trying to look, with one eye, over this couple's shoulder to find the tea I wanted, when from across the coffee shop came John. He had spotted me struggling to keep my balance and find the tea I wanted, while working my way around the chatting couple to get it. He said, "What can I do for you? What are you looking for? How can I help you?" He got the tea for me and got me back to the counter. I was so impressed with his manners, going over and above his job description to help a customer like me, or to even notice a customer like me. I've always wanted to tell him that during my recovery Peet's was not a coffee shop to me, Peet's was like coming home. As soon as I got in there and sat down, I was like, "Ahh, here I am." I could rest, relax; I didn't have to be doing anything and I didn't have to talk to anyone in my whispery voice.

John and everyone else who worked there knew I talked in a whisper. As soon as I ordered something they would lean forward to hear me; they knew I couldn't talk louder without going into coughing spasms. In these ways and more, Peet's really was my home away from home. This great place really helped my recovery, especially knowing they were there and had my back while I visited. If anything went wrong, I knew they'd take care of it. Peet's was an important piece of my recovery puzzle.

Now that I was driving myself, I was absolutely delighted to be back at Peet's every day to see what I considered my friends: the people that worked there, the people tapping on lap tops, all of the coffee breakers who showed up every day at the same time. There was one lady clearly writing a book. I never knew their names, I just knew they were all there when I was, and it felt like one big family. I was home in my house, so to speak.

Email sent on 1/7/2010

Saw the Neuro Ophthalmologist
today. (Who even knew that was a
specialty?) Dr. McCaully and a Dr.
Hoyt. 2 hour appt.

The third nerve is still trying to
heal so my eyelid can open. Seems
the nerve splits in the back of
the eye. Part of it is working
because my eye can go from side to
side. The other part of it makes
the eye go up and down. That part
is not working.

Apparently what can happen is the
eye lid pops open and the eye
looks down but stays looking down.
The doctors feel that one day,
between 6-9 months after my Oct.
28th surgery, the lid will open.
It will just depend on what the
eye does at that point, which they
can't predict. They also say
surgery can correct this and it is
good the lid is still closed
because it protects the retina
right now. They can't say for sure
that I won't have double vision
for the rest of my life. That
remains to be seen, but they
aren't pessimistic. They reiterate
that this is a long healing
process for the nerves and there
is just no predicting what may
happen or when. They have given me

some scenarios that could happen but then again, the lid could open and all is fine.

One of the docs I saw, Dr. Hoyt, has been at UCSF as a teaching doc for 50 years. Super guy, and at that age he has seen almost every outcome from this surgery that there is (his words) and yet he still can't predict what or how I might heal.

So let the healing continue!—T

Email sent out on 1/12/2010

Radiology

Met with oncologist/radiologist today, Dr. Igor Barani. We continue to be so impressed with the docs at UCSF.

He's scheduling another MRI for some time in Jan. Then we can see how the leftover tumor pieces that are still there are doing. Apparently with this type of tumor, once you cut away at it, it can, in rare cases, become a fast growing tumor.

The MRI will tell us if it has turned into fast growing. If it

has, then he needs to start 5 1/2
weeks of daily radiation to zap
it. This results in complete
exhaustion for me apparently along
with other risks that radiation
can bring, although not so many
now that they can focus the beam
so well, but I could get memory
loss, loss of eye sight in my
right eye, cognitive problems,
etc.

The doctor is hoping the scan will
show us that it has remained slow
growing. If that is the case, we
have opted to watch and wait. He
said he draws a line in the sand
of when the tumor is encroaching
on this or that and at that point
I will need radiation.

I asked if it was a given that I
would eventually get to that line
in the sand and he said yes. It
could be months or years. There is
no more risk in the future then
there is now with the radiation.

We're thinking we'll watch and
wait, which is his recommendation
also. Techniques will only get
more refined and with more
research who knows what might be
available treatment-wise.

So unless the MRI shows the tumor growing quite fast, we're on a every 3 month MRI scan schedule.—T

Email sent on 1/20/2010

Had MRI's over the weekend to start charting the growth of the pieces of tumor that are left. They were concerned that this tumor can morph into a fast growing tumor, rare, but it can happen.

Good news is that has not happened. Tumor pieces haven't changed since the last surgery Oct. 28. So now we'll do an MRI scan every 3 months. At some point it will cross a line (and he said yes, I will get to the line at some point), then we will do radiation to beat it back.

I will never get rid of all of it. We can only beat it back with radiation periodically.

Am also enrolling in a national study with UCSF for this type of tumor. They are looking for DNA markers that can identify people who might have the marker for getting this tumor. Very excited

that maybe I can contribute
something to someone else. —T

Chapter 13 Ricochet

Acupuncture treatments were instrumental in keeping my mood elevated and aiding in getting my balance back for walking.

At first I was going once a week. Then it turned into once every two weeks. Currently I go four or five times a year to get tuned up for seasonal changes. Seasonal tune ups keep our bodies in sync with changes in weather, daylight, temperature, etc. Previously, when I needed a treatment, Don had to drive me, drop me off, hang out and wait for me to be done, and then bring me back home. When I was finally able to drive myself, not only did it free him up, but I enjoyed a sense of accomplishment being able to do it myself.

I scheduled my first drive down the freeway when it was not rush hour so I wouldn't have to deal with traffic. I drove down, parked, walked in, and had my acupuncture treatment. No problems. Since my car had blind spots on either side and I had a blind spot on my right side because my closed eye, I always made sure to scan side to side. My left eye could only look so far to the right, so I was careful to really scan that side, making sure nobody was coming across a crosswalk, no cars were pulling out from driveways on that side, or any other obstructions were in view. My head was like a swivel the whole time I drove, making sure I could see the entire view, and not just the view out of one eye.

Often during my acupuncture treatments, my acupuncturist, Marty would say, "Wow, you have a huge bruise on your leg. How did you get that?" Or maybe, "There is a very large bruise on your arm. How did you get that?"

My answer each and every time was, "I don't know." I didn't know because I ricocheted through life. My balance was still off as I walked through my house, through crowds of people, wherever and whenever. I bumped into things, bounced off them, and continued on. My rug loom is very huge and takes up a large space at one end of our living room. I constantly bumped into that, bounced off it, and moved on.

I got so I didn't pay attention to what I was bouncing off of because it happened so often. Because I was on a baby aspirin and Plavix daily due to previous heart attacks, I bruised easily. I was used to bruising easily; I just hadn't bumped into things before quite like I did now.

Ricocheting through life became a theme of my existence, and when I set out to write this book, the title. In our own ways, we all ricochet through life, but sharing my bump-filled journey here, and how I continued on, has become an important part of my healing process.

I remember one time in San Francisco, going to an estate sale with my mom. We were coming into a complicated intersection, where five streets came together at varying angles at the stoplight. A guy in a van sped across 4 lanes of traffic from a side street near the intersection, and there was no way I could track him that quickly. Even if I had been scanning (which I'm sure I was) it all happened so fast. Had it not been for my mom spotting him and alerting me, I would have hit him. It wouldn't have been my fault, but it wouldn't have mattered. Her warning allowed me to jerk my head in the van's direction, put the brakes on, and avoid an accident. That was the closest I came to having an accident due to my physical blind spot.

Once I started getting acupuncture on a regular basis, I told my son, Jasen, in Portland, how awesome it was, and all the things it helped with…my mood, my balance, my limited hearing in my right ear, hip pain from laying in the same position for ten hours just to mention a few. He was having some health issues. I told him, "They can help with all that."

Jasen wasn't happy with the doctors he was finding and the answers he was getting regarding his health. He had Gird (acid reflux) and had been given drugs to help with that. He also had an enlarged prostate but was discouraged his doctors kept putting him on medication. It seemed the only solution he was offered was prescription medication, and it sounded as though he'd have to stay on drugs for life. Jasen wanted answers, not prescriptions.

I asked my acupuncturist, Marty, if he knew anybody up in Portland. He looked through the list of acupuncturists who had joined the national society, and gave me a couple of names, although he didn't know any of them personally.

Jasen was getting a regular massage, weekly, and in that same studio was an acupuncturist, named David Tircuit. Jasen made an appointment and after his first visit, called me, blown away. It turns out that David does more than just acupuncture. He is also trained in Qigong.

First he takes your pulse, as they all do, the Chinese way, then he'll put in the acupuncture needles, and then he lays his hands on you, and basically moves energy around. Very hocus pocus is how it sounded to me. Jasen has always been super curious about how things work so he was watching David. As Jasen lay on the table, he watched everything that David did. When David would lay his hand on Jasen's hip, and another hand on the shoulder to line up the energy, David's eyes would roll back in his head.

Jasen's was concerned about David and said, "Oh my God, are you all right man?" Apparently David looked like he might pass out. It must take a lot of energy or a lot of focus to move the energy around in someone else's body.

Jasen said "Oh my God, Mom, you've got to come up, you've got to come up, you've got to see this guy. This guy's awesome. I think he can get your eye open. Please, please, come up and see this guy."

I had originally booked a trip after Christmas 2009 to fly up and see them. About two days before the trip, I started feeling like I might be catching a cold. There was no way I wanted to get on an airplane and get sicker, so I ended up cancelling that trip. What I couldn't sort out at that time was, was I really getting sick, or was I just afraid to fly and travel by myself? I didn't have the answer at that time, but looking back on it, I believe I was afraid to fly. I was afraid I couldn't handle all the people moving around me, and all the commotion in an airport. Would I be able to find my way to the gate, the plane, baggage claim? Sure my brain seemed to be working well, but traveling meant putting myself in unfamiliar surroundings. I hadn't yet subjected myself to a place where I didn't know how to find places and things I needed. I think I cancelled that trip because I was just afraid to fly and travel alone.

Email sent 4/13/2010

Latest MRI Scan

Just came from my Radiology Oncologist. He has reviewed my MRI from last week and said there is absolutely no growth in the tumor pieces that are still in there.

He also said there is no need for radiology at this time and I might not need it for a couple of years.

He wants to continue to do MRI's
every 3 months....at least for
this year. But said based on what
he's seeing, he would recommend
gamma knife radiation rather than
generalized radiation. The gamma
knife if very focused and
basically nukes the spot they are
going after. Rather than 5-6 weeks
of radiation 5 days a week, it
appears when it needs to be done
it will be a 1 day event.

He also is very excited about a
new gamma knife machine they are
getting in Aug. that will allow
him to do even more focused
radiation. Crazy how this works. I
bet he's really good at video
games! This is mostly done thru
robotics that he manipulates. The
new machine allows him to get
within 1 mm of a critical nerve,
etc.

So far so good. He told me to quit
feeling like a patient. Said I've
made a remarkable recovery and to
get on with my life. Yahoo! —T

Chapter 14 Live Until You Use up the Toothpaste

I didn't make my first long trip until spring, 2010, when I went down to see my Dad in South Texas. I felt it was really important to make this trip for my dad's sake. I couldn't imagine being a dad and having your only daughter go through brain tumor surgery and not be able to be there.

My stepmother had been ill for so long and my dad was her only caretaker. I knew he couldn't leave to come and be with me. I kept in touch with him as often as I could during the surgeries, and Don updated him constantly. But I felt it must have been really hard for him to be that far away from me during my surgeries and recoveries. Either instance could have been the last time he saw me alive.

I couldn't talk to my dad on the phone because he had a hearing problem, and I had no voice. He was 86 at the time. Every time I would call I couldn't do more than whisper, and he couldn't hear me. I could

e-mail him to keep him updated, but my dad
didn't understand how to hit reply. He read
my e-mails, he just didn't write back. If I
wrote something to him that he had a
question about, he'd have to call.

To get to McAllen, Texas, I flew into
Houston, changed planes, and then flew to
McAllen. I decided to use frequent flyer
miles and book myself a first class seat
because I didn't want to be back in coach
in case something went wrong and I needed
help quickly. I wanted to be able to fall
into the aisle, or raise my hand or
something, and have somebody see me. The
whole family knew I was flying that day.
What if the plane was late? What if the
flight was cancelled? What if I had to go
to a hotel? Everybody was concerned.

The first leg of the flight went just
fine. I'd been through the Houston airport
many times and was able to find my way
around without any problems.

As I walked to my gate for the next
flight, I called my son and said, "Hey

Jasen, here I am in Houston" and at that point I burst into tears.

"Oh my God, Mom, is everything ok? Are you able to find your way? Where are you? What's going on?"

I said, "Everything's fine Jasen. I'm so relieved that I'm able to do this, that my brain is okay, and I'm able to find my way around, negotiate all the people and loudspeakers, and noise. I can actually still do this. I can still see the world."

He was relieved that everything had gone fine. I got down to my Dad's just fine, and negotiated the trip home too. In the spring of 2010 I became part of the flying public again.

In April of that year, I travelled up to Portland to see Jasen's acupuncturist, David. I had never had a Qigong experience before and was warily looking forward to it. One of the side effects of my surgery was not being able to take a deep breath. I could breathe fine when I walked around normally, but I wasn't able to breathe deeply while relaxing or meditating without going into a coughing spasm. I'd get a tickle in the back of my throat, try to direct my breathing past, or around it, and not be able to.

Jasen suggested I try and focus on that little tickle and see if I could get it to relax. I had a little success with that, but as of April 2010, I was still unable to take a deep breath. I felt that tickle almost 24-hours a day, although as long as I didn't take a deep breath, it didn't affect me. Sometimes food would bump into "it" and I'd end up with another coughing spasm.

Jasen had explained to David what was going on with me, and what I'd been through. David had been working on keeping Jasen's stress level down concerning his mother's brain-tumor surgery.

When I arrived David first put in the acupuncture needles, then he placed one of his hands on my right hip, and the other on my right shoulder. I didn't watch him the way Jasen had, so I didn't see whether his eyes rolled back in his head like he was going to pass out. As I lay there, I could feel the tickle go away, and a muscle moved deep in my throat.

I believe there really is something to Qigong, that David did move energy. Whatever he did, it made that tickle go away, and nobody else had been able to do that. As soon as I noticed it was gone, which was almost immediately, I took a deep breath. For the first time since September 2009, I was able to breathe deeply again. David continued to place his hands in various positions, lower down on my leg and on my head, for example, but whatever energy he moved when he touched my hip and shoulder, made that tickle go away.

What I didn't know was whether it would stay away, or come back. When we were done with the treatment, I left with tears in my eyes. Being able to breathe deeply again was so huge to me.

I called Don in my trying-to-talk, whispery, hiccupping-while-crying voice and said, "Oh my, for the first time since my surgeries I'm able to take a deep breath again. The tickle is gone."

Happily, it has pretty much stayed gone. Sometimes when I swallow, or talk too long without pausing to swallow, or take too many deep breaths, it will come back. But for the most part, I can now take deep breaths. I can take enough of them to get relaxed, and get into ~~the~~ guided imagery or meditation, or whatever else I'm trying to do. Whatever David did, it worked.

During another visit later that April of 2010, I was there for a very short time and David didn't have any appointments open. I had taken my grandson Lucas up there for the weekend, so he could hang out with his cousin and her family, Chris and Scotty, Ella and George. Since I couldn't get in with David, I booked a massage with a woman named Misty. I'd wanted to start getting massages at home, thinking they might help. I'd never had a massage. Since Jasen and Allison were so high on Misty, I thought, "Well, I'll have a massage up there, then I'll know what a good one feels like and I can try to find somebody at home."

Misty gave me a great massage, very relaxing. A day later, Lucas and I got back on the plane. At some point, I turned to Lucas to say something, still speaking in a whisper, and an actual voice came out. He didn't notice that I'd spoken in an actual voice, but I was stunned. I found that for the rest of my trip from Portland to Oakland, I could switch between my whisper voice and my actual voice. Sadly, I lost the ability to switch back and forth within a couple of weeks. My actual voice was not strong, and most people said it didn't even sound like me, but at least people could hear me. I could call my dad and he could hear me.

From then on, almost every time one of the kids called, they would say, "Wow your voice is so much stronger than the last time I heard it."

Just slowly, slowly, slowly; through acupuncture, through deep breathing, maybe through exercise (I was walking a mile to two miles a day) slowly, slowly, my voice came back. I think it had something to do with the massage up in Portland. I believe Misty got rid of some of the toxins that were still in my body from the surgeries, maybe released some muscles in my throat and vocal chords, allowing my voice to come back. Don disagreed, feeling that it was complete happenstance. But with all I've been through, I don't believe in happenstance. I think that all the praying, all the work I've done, all the doctors I've reached out to, all the alternative medicine people I've seen, keeps coming into me and going through me, and creating changes, getting me back to my normal.

The massage was the trigger that pulled all of what everyone else had been doing, together, and gave me my voice back. Doctors hadn't been able to tell me for sure that my voice would ever come back. I have been and still am a daily work in progress. I'm told I am the poster child for my doctors. They are all stunned by the progress I've made, and also by the side-effects that did not happen to me.

I'm told, based on their moving and lifting of my brain during surgery, that I could easily have emerged unable to walk again, perhaps with severe brain damage. I never let those things cross my mind before surgery. I focused on all things positive. I selected the top surgeons and hospital in the world for my surgery, and I let all things positive come together to carry me through this. Never walk again? Not a chance. Severe brain damage? Too much guided imagery and attitude preparation went into this before the surgery for that to happen.

My acupuncturist, Marty Rossman, was responsible for guiding my alternative medicine treatments, even though it wasn't something we ever discussed and he didn't have any agenda or even any thought about doing it. I think that when I was there, it would pop into his head though, and he would say, "Hey, have you ever done this? Have you ever done that?"

I was in for an appointment with Marty in the spring of 2010 and he said, "Have you ever had cranial sacral work done?" I

had never heard of it. The only two
alternative medicine things I'd ever heard
of were massage therapy, and acupuncture. I
was a newbie to alternative medicine stuff.
I answered, "No I've never had cranial
sacral work." He said, "I think it can
help with the numbness and tightness that
you feel on the right side of your face,
because the mastoid muscle is crunched down
and yanking your jaw way to the right,
pulling your teeth and causing your jaw to
be misaligned." I had tried acupuncture to
loosen that muscle and get it to relax, but
without success. Marty explained that he
had a practitioner named Pat, who came into
his office and did cranial sacral work. I
got her phone number and made an
appointment.

Now, I live with an orthopedic surgeon
as a husband; all this stuff is like hocus
pocus to him. I never mentioned that I was
going for cranial sacral work. I just told
him I had an appointment at Marty's that
Friday afternoon and he didn't think
anything of it. I picked my battles

carefully with the alternative medicine issues.

Pat also did some guided imagery with me as she did the cranial sacral work. I don't think that in my entire life, I have ever felt that relaxed. I experienced a total letting go of my mind and body; a complete relaxation. It was a very interesting experience. I happened to mention it to Don's daughter, Elizabeth, who I had originally thrown off my boat, but was now back on riding the waves with me. She was a massage therapist and said, "Sure I know cranial sacral. I've been doing it for years." Why should I drive a half hour down the freeway to have this done, when my stepdaughter does it?

I switched to Elizabeth. We both agreed to the sessions while Don worked on Mondays, and neither one of us would mention it to him. We knew he would be really, really upset with all the hocus pocus that I was doing. No point in upsetting his apple cart until we knew if I was going to get any benefit from this.

Elizabeth combined the cranial sacral work along with some massage, mostly on my right side, trying to loosen up muscles that had clamped down. My skull was like a rock. I couldn't even push the skin around on my head. If I took my fist and knocked on my head, it felt like I had a wooden head.

Muscles will do this in response to surgery. It is a protective mechanism in the body. Maybe because I had two 10-hour surgeries so close together, the muscles just never unclamped. My right neck muscle was super tight too, because my closed right eye caused me to turn my head in an abnormal manner. I didn't look to the right since I knew I couldn't see anything anyway. It wasn't a conscious decision not to look to the right. My body just gets trained by the monocular vision. Without use in that direction, my neck started to stiffen.

Every week she would work on my neck and try and keep it from stiffening up. We made a little progress, but during the week it would crunch back down again. We were able to loosen the skin that was so tight on the skull. Finally I could push it around pretty freely. My jaw was still way off; we weren't making any progress on that, but even still, the cranial sacral sessions were very relaxing and very calming.

Chapter 15 Use the Whole Sidewalk

I felt definite benefits from the cranial sacral sessions with Elizabeth. My hip pain would periodically go away. I started having "fuzzy feet." Out of nowhere, the bottoms of my feet felt fuzzy. One of my doctors asked me, "Does it feel like when you tie your shoelaces too tight and your feet start to go to sleep?" It was something like that, yes. I would get a tingling feeling just above my kneecap sometimes too, but mostly in the bottom of my feet.

Elizabeth worked on that issue to make sure I had good circulation going on throughout my body. When she moved to focusing on my feet, we made some huge discoveries. Her massage of the feet alleviated the fuzziness and brought a huge improvement in my balance. I became less wobbly on my feet and started to focus on how I was walking.

Rather than putting my foot down heel to toe, I was dropping my whole foot down

at one time, in a "plop, plop" way. I think
I might have feared that I needed as much
of my foot down as quickly as possible to
stay upright and walking. Not so any
longer.

Elizabeth suggested that I start
focusing on a heel-then-toe placement,
which ended up having a huge impact on my
balance. Through her suggestions and work,
Elizabeth showed me how to walk again. It
was a big turning point in my journey.

Sometime during the late summer of
2010 I got tired of hiding the fact that I
was going to my husband's daughter for
these treatments. I told Don that Elizabeth
had been working on me for a couple of
months, and that her treatments were making
a difference. I was walking better and my
balance was better. Elizabeth had also
noticed that when I walked, I tended to
hunch over and look down. She said,
"Straighten up and look straight ahead." I
believe this tendency to look down came
from my fear of falling. It had been
drilled into me, "You can't fall, you can't
fall, you can't fall." With my balance so

poor and my vision not great, I didn't have
a lot of depth perception.

Sidewalks were particularly
troublesome because I didn't always see the
unevenness of them. Looking down kept me
from tripping and falling. Since my
treatments with Elizabeth, I've learned to
trust the feeling in the bottom of my feet
and let it guide me more than my vision.
Feeling with the bottom of my feet when I
walked, allowed me to look forward at the
sidewalk; and see if something looks like
it's not the same height, or if there's a
bump or a rock in the road, or whatever,
then at that point I can do a quick
downward glance to make sure I avoid it.
Otherwise I keep my vision forward. This
new and more correct way of walking is
something I occasionally have to remind
myself to do— don't bend over; don't keep
looking down. Raising my head and looking
ahead meant more to me than regaining my
balance, it became a physical affirmation
that I was ready to face forward and move
on.

Telling Don about my cranial sacral sessions with Elizabeth was about more than just sharing my improvements. I wanted him to know that western medicine didn't have all the answers. As an Army doctor stationed in Japan, Don did see the benefits of acupuncture, and while I don't think he's ever had an acupuncture treatment, he's never had a problem with me getting one.

For the most part though, Don considered most alternative medicine hocus pocus. I needed him to know that even though alternative medicine couldn't necessarily diagnose, and certainly didn't do surgery, it had a place in my treatment protocol. There is no doubt that Western medicine saved my life by getting rid of most of my tumor. I wasn't throwing Western medicine out of my bag of tricks, but at this point Western medicine had no specific answers to improve the leftover conditions from my surgery.

The other reason I wanted Don to know about the cranial sacral treatments was, of course, to share my improvement. He had already noticed how much better I was doing and how much better my balance was. I wanted him to know that he wasn't the only healer in the family; that his daughter was quite skilled and knowledgeable in her own right. I wanted him to know what a huge asset she'd been for me. I appreciated everything she'd done and everything she had brought to our sessions, whether it worked or not.

It has been amazing to me how well my brain has accommodated my monocular vision. I have learned to trust my brain and let it accommodate. For instance, my brain has used the shadows on the sidewalk to let me know that the sidewalk is uneven. I've now done enough driving that my brain has learned how far away I am from the car on my right. When I first started driving again, I knew exactly how far everything on my left was, but it took some time to get beyond my "blind spot" on the right. Until then, I stayed closer to the left side of the lane to create an allowance for the person on the right.

I learned a variety of little tricks to accommodate my monocular vision. Initially, I wouldn't pull into a parking space between two cars. Instead, I'd park way out where there were plenty of empty spaces. One day I realized that I didn't need to look at the cars, I could look at the painted lines on the ground. As long as I kept close to the parking space line on the left, I'd be fine on the right. What a revelation! I could now park anywhere.

I became more confident that my brain would figure out things that had been frustrating me for years.

I could either stay as the "new" Mom 3.0 (as my son called me), new and updated version, or I could figure out ways and methods to work with the problems I had, and see if I couldn't resolve some of them.

Email sent on 4/20/2010

Neuro Eye Doc

Just back from UCSF. The doc is not all that optimistic about my eye opening. He said he could connect the lid to the eyebrow and

I could open it that way. But then
we checked my double vision with
that eye open, and even using the
strongest lens available, I still
had double vision. I can have eye
surgery and a doc can line up the
right eye with the left so as long
as I look straight ahead, I won't
have double vision. But the
surgery can only be done once.
After that there is scar tissue
that would prevent it from being
done again. So if the nerves are
still healing and moving the eye
around even 1 mm, then the surgery
would fix it only for a short time
and then I'd be out of alignment
again.

Don told him when he checks my eye
for peripheral vision (Don) felt
like it continued to improve.

My depth of field test improved
this time also.

So all of us agreed to wait longer
(3-6 more months) and see if it
won't open on its own or if the
double vision might just improve
to where it can be corrected with
lenses.

So not the best of news but not
the worst either. —T

Email sent 6/4/2010

Bump in the Road

Looks like I'll be starting
radiation treatment this next Wed.
Here are the details:

Last evening, all of sudden, my
head felt really big, as did my
closed eye and my right ear. Since
none were swollen, it seemed like
it was just pressure from the
inside. I couldn't discount that
it also might have been just a
bunch of nerves reconnecting all
at once.

So we waited a few days to see
what these symptoms might progress
into. Nothing changed. Don did an
eye exam yesterday and my field of
vision in my right eye was half
what it was a month ago. Hearing
did seem to be the same. But when
he asked that I open my mouth
wide, I could not form an 'o' nor
an oval. The only way I could open
it was pull down on the right
side.

So we immediately got on the phone
to all my docs. I also had a blood
test that showed elevated
something or other in the
pituitary gland (most likely from

piece of tumor pressing on the gland).

Long and short of it is some time this weekend I'll go in for another MRI so they can isolate what is happening. Their best guess is one of 2 things. Either the tumor pieces have now morphed into fast growing or a tumor piece has moved or grown enough that it is pressing on the brain stem. I'll go in on Monday and spend much of the day with docs and having measurements done so they can start to play 'video games' in my head on Wed. with radiation. The measurements line everything up for them so that when they 'shoot', they get what they want.

Not sure if this will be radiation I need every day or if it will be gamma knife radiation which would be once a week. Either radiation is for about 5 weeks....at least for this go round.

They all did feel and agree that surgery would not be done now. That now we were to the point where radiation was the most effective option because the tumor pieces are just too small or too close to optic nerves, etc. to be able to get with surgery.

Will keep all posted as we learn
more. —T

Email Sent 6/7/2010

After seeing all the docs today
and getting a CT scan, I'm all set
to start radiation on Wed. at 2.
It will be done every day, 20 min.
per day, for 5 1/2-6 weeks.

Turns out that a pretty good piece
of tumor was left in because it
was too dangerous to do surgery
on. It's sitting on the carotid
artery and wrapped around the
optic nerve. There was no way they
could go after this during
surgery. They had hoped it would
behave itself and not cause any
problems for a while.

It has not grown, but shifted
enough that it is now pressing on
the artery and compressing too
much on the optic nerve. It's time
to zap it. Meanwhile, the MRI this
weekend showed that all the other
tumor bits that were left in are
not growing and are the same as
the last scan....so that's great
news.

The radiation will kill this
tumor. He said it kills the cells

in the tumor, the body then washes
out all those cells but the
skin/shell of the tumor remains.
But without all the cells inside
it, it's no longer heavy and
causing a problem.

He will focus the radiation on the
tumor but there could be some
spillover to the pituitary gland
and the hypothalamus. Depending on
how the glands handle it, it could
be they get slightly damaged and I
end up on medication for life, to
replace what the radiation zapped
out of them. Easily treatable he
said.

He is confident this will kill
this tumor but my neuro surgeon
doc said he was not confident this
would allow my eye lid to open. He
feels that at some point I will
need plastic surgery to attach it
to my eyebrow and then I'll be
able to open the eye by lifting
the eyebrow. But we'll give it a
year to two to see if it can't
open on its own.

They said side effects are perhaps
hair loss (not likely he said),
fatigue (but not debilitating),
and perhaps some memory loss. So
he's referred me to a
neuropsychologist to do a mental
workup now and then we'll do

another workup after the radiation to see if any memory/mental problems occurred. The fatigue is cumulative so doesn't really start hitting you too much until the 5th or 6th week apparently. Plus I'll be using acupuncture. Marty says he gets great results with radiation fatigue and he has a nutritionist on staff who also has some great ideas to help with the fatigue.

So all around, I should be in good hands and not be slowed down too much by this at all.....just a bump in the road to the rest of my life!—T

My mom gave Don and me each a handmade calendar so we could cross off each day that radiation was finished. It would be a good visual way to see that we were progressing to an end point.

Email sent 6/24/2010

Brain Update

For the past 2 days, I have been meeting with the neuropsychologist. She's been testing each part of the brain

with various diagnostic tests,
checking to see if, because of the
surgeries, there is any loss of
brain functions in any section of
the brain.

During the surgeries, there were
times the surgeons had to move
certain lobes of the brain aside
to get to pieces of the tumor.
Brain lobes often react poorly to
this movement.

After completing all the testing,
the doc said I'm doing fabulous.
Usually once she finishes her
report, she has recommendations
that the patient see another doc
to work on brain function, maybe a
psychologist for mood and
depression, etc.

Her recommendations for me: She
had none. She said it's been a
long time since she tested a
patient that's doing this well.
She always has recommendations.
But because my brain is
functioning so well and my mood
and spirits are good, she said
just go live your life as you are.
You're doing great!

Wow....what a huge relief. We felt
here at home that everything
seemed fine and I seemed to be
functioning fine. But thought

maybe there were some small subtle changes that maybe we weren't picking up on.—T

The doctors had originally wanted to do all of the diagnostic work in one day. The testing, before it started, seemed really stressful to me. It was similar testing to what I had done on students for years as a Reading Specialist in the public schools. Now, here I was, the tables turned. I was the testee.

As a result, I asked that they break up the testing into two days. That seemed much more manageable to me and not nearly as stressful.

I wasn't stressed out much by the idea of receiving radiation. Again, I felt that I had one of the best doctors in the world and I was being treated at one of the top facilities in the world. I could have made my daily treatment easier if I'd opted to have the radiation done at Marin Community Hospital which was only 15 minutes from our house. But both Don and I wanted to stay with the team of doctors at UCSF. Don was willing to drive me in five days a week for the radiation, so that's what we did.

The first thing the doctors ask during these radiation treatments is to not move at all or they will have trouble focusing the beams. I received a mesh mask to place over my face. The mask was initially made by pressing warm plastic over my face to create a perfect outline. Then my head was anchored to the table using the base of the mask. I couldn't move my head up, down, left, or right. The purpose of the mask was to hold my head in place during radiation treatments. I hadn't known in advance that they were going to do this. Being a little bit claustrophobic, I had to center myself and say, "Okay take a deep breath because you're going to be trapped in here every day for six weeks."

I expected to be completely exhausted from the radiation, to the point of being like a zombie. I expected that I'd go in every day, get the treatment, come home and sleep all day and night; go in the next day for the treatment, and repeat the same process, possibly sleeping the whole weekend. Just the trip into the city every day and back, 45 minutes each way, another 15 minutes to park plus walking into the place, seemed exhausting.

It was **quite a trek** each day.

Don drove me in because we knew I was going to be tired. Dr. Barani kept emphasizing, "Don't let her drive during this time." I did continue to drive, not to the treatments, but around town. However, driving into the city, over the Golden Gate Bridge, maneuvering in all that traffic was likely to be too much for me, so Don did that. Each of his daughters, Kathy and Elizabeth, were also kind enough to drive me on two occasions, but the rest of the six weeks, five days a week, Don trucked me in and trucked me back.

Radiation treatments were not as exhausting as I had feared. For the first week I would come home and lay down. I never fell asleep; I wasn't that tired. I wanted to make sure I wasn't using up energy that might be better used to get through the radiation. I didn't want to do too much. Since I had to go through this treatment, I wanted to make sure I got the full benefit of it, and didn't waste any of it by tiring myself needlessly.

After the first week, I gave up laying down every day. Dr. Barani had me on steroids to stop my brain stem from swelling. Steroids make it hard to sleep, so I opted not to sleep during the day in order to get the most out of my nighttime sleep.

I would say after about two, to two and a half weeks, I did start to feel a little fatigued, although it certainly wasn't overwhelming. I could still go out every morning, drive to the coffee shop, read my newspaper, come back home, and package some books (because we're rare book dealers). I could even weave a little in the afternoon. There wasn't anything I couldn't manage because of the radiation treatments.

On one of the first treatment days, I sat in the waiting room, my head back, my eyes closed, just resting. Don had been sitting right next to me.

Suddenly I heard him out in the hallway, sounding really excited about meeting someone. I opened my eyes and saw him in the hallway talking to a young woman, giving her a hug, big smiles from both of them.

He introduced her as Lisa Mannheimer-Miller, a patient he'd operated on back when she was a teenager and had dislocated her head from her spinal column.

I looked at him like he was nuts. How could he be saying this and yet this young woman was standing here, alive, looking and smiling at me? If what he just told me about her was true, she'd be dead.

Apparently Lisa had crashed her car through a front yard fence. The paramedic on the scene knew that if he put her in a neck brace, he'd break the bond between her head and her spinal column. Instead, he eased her onto a backboard and transported her to the hospital.

Don was on call that night. The
neurosurgeon on duty showed Don the x-rays
without comment, letting Don form his own
opinion.

Don pointed out that her head was
displaced from her spinal column. Both of
them knew that if they tried to line it
back up, it was instant death for her.

Don went to the library to do some
quick research but couldn't find any
medical literature on how to survive this
kind of injury, nor was there a medical
procedure suggested. After consulting the
neurologist, they decided to try to wire
everything in place just as it was. That's
what they did. This young woman is living
proof that it had worked.

Maybe that's why I was there, so these
two could reconnect. After she had been
discharged from the hospital he never knew
what became of her.

Lisa's accident turned her life
around. She decided to dedicate her life to
helping people. She became a nurse at the
Radiology/Oncology unit at UCSF. She is a

walking miracle with a wonderful husband and beautiful daughter. She took her second chance at life and ran with it big time. She and her family now have a permanent place in our hearts and family.

Lisa said that just that morning she had been wondering about Dr. Seymour, hoping to one day find him, and now here he was, right in front of her. They were both in tears. She had managed to locate the paramedic who was on the scene that night, and it meant a lot for her to be able to thank him.

One day, in the grocery store, a lady came up to her and said, "I think I know you."

"Yes," said Lisa, "I'm the young woman that crashed through your fence that night."

Her stories of finding all the pieces of her puzzle still give me chills. My thought at that time was, "So this is why I'm here for radiation, at this moment in time, at this hospital. For the coming together of these two people."

Chapter 16 Stunning

Every Friday after treatment Don and I met with Dr. Barani. When we met with him the first week, I asked him why did he meet with us every Friday

He said, "We're just here to support you and encourage you, and anything we can do for you, that's what we're here for."

The second week I asked him, "Do some people quit?"

"Oh yeah, lots of people quit; they start their treatment, and they just quit."

"Well, if that's why you're meeting with me every Friday, you don't need to bother, because I'm not quitting. Once you mentally decide to do this, I can't imagine why anyone would quit. This isn't something that doctors recommend lightly, and if you recommended it, you clearly feel like I better have it or my health may be in danger, my life may be in danger. Why on earth would somebody quit?"

He said, "It happens all the time."

I didn't quit. We continued on for six weeks. By the end of the six weeks, I was pretty tired. I was on steroids the entire six weeks. Once we finished I was able to get off them. I started sleeping well again and feeling rested.

Six months after radiation ended, I no longer felt the effects of radiation at all. It gradually left my system during that time period. Every day I felt a little bit better and stronger. I remember being out in our back yard one day doing some yard work and thinking, wow, I don't feel one bit tired. The radiation event had passed.

After radiation ended, my mom and I flew up to Portland to celebrate Austen's, (Jasen's daughter) birthday. Her birthday is in June but since I had to do the radiation treatments, I was unable to go up to Portland in June.

Shortly after arriving, this precious little three-year-old walked up and stood in front of me, put her little hand over my closed eye and said: "When I grow up, I'm going to be an eye doctor and I will fix your eye."

WOW! What Three-year-old thinks in these terms, or has enough compassion and vocabulary to be able to express this?

My closed eye had always been of huge interest to her ever since the surgeries. The rest of my grandchildren never mentioned it. I told all of them that if they ever had any questions or wanted to talk to me about my experiences, to please feel free.

But each and every time I saw Austen after the surgeries, she always asked: "When will the doctors fix your eye?"

I guess by age three she'd had enough. To heck with the doctors, she'd just grow up, become an eye doctor and fix it herself.

Chapter 17 Mike After Mass

In January, 2011, Don told me that an acquaintance named Mike at his church needed radiation treatment and was refusing it.

I asked, "Why?"

Don said, "He won't tell us, but he's told the doctors he's not going to do it."

I told Don I'd be happy to talk to Mike about my experiences.

Don arranged a meeting and when I sat down with Mike, I said, "If you're thinking this is going to make you really, really tired, as in zombie tired; it won't. That was my concern too; that for six weeks I would be completely out of it and sleep around the clock. It's nothing like that." I explained that by the end of the six weeks I felt a little fatigue, but I wasn't ever in zombie mode. I also shared that my biggest concern was how I was going to take care of myself when I was so exhausted, and how that turned out not to be a problem.

Mike went ahead and got the radiation.

I saw him again in October 2012. He came up to me, gave me a big hug, and said, "I owe my life to you because I would not have gotten that radiation if you hadn't taken the time to come in and talk to me." He added, "I did think it was going to leave me completely exhausted and I didn't know how I was going to take care of myself. I didn't want to be a burden on anybody else in the family. I'm just so grateful."

Email Sent on 7/20/2010

Treatments Done!

Met with the doctor today after treatment was over. I'll see him again in 30 days.

He said it can take 6 months for the swelling to go down after radiation treatment. The swelling to the tumor. Radiation apparently really causes a fair amount of swelling and it's slow to go down. Takes up to a year for the body to absorb the tumor tissue. He said gradually over the next 6 months the symptoms I've had, numbness on right side of head, crackling in

my ear (fluid in the right ear),
head feeling 'big', jaw
misaligned....should gradually
start to go away.

He's most excited about the fluid
in the inner ear. He said that's
the best sign that the radiation
did its job and killed the tumor.
He said if I had never gotten the
crackling sound he would have been
very concerned. So he's super
excited all will be well. MRI in 3
months will tell us more.

So glad to be done with the daily
trips. All very tiring. Be nice
not to feel tired all the time.—T

Email sent 10/29/2010

Wed MRI

MRI is back from Wed. No changes
from the radiation show up yet.
That's what my doc thought we'd
see at this point. Tumor is not
growing so that's great. If
nothing else, we stopped it in its
tracks. He said at 6 month's MRI,
in January we should see then that
it is dead.

Email sent 11/12/2010

MRI Follow-up

Met with my radiology-oncology
doctor today for follow-up after
the MRI. He is most pleased with
the MRI. He said the report is
always great but the doctor that
is treating the patient can often
see more in the scan than the
radiologist reading the report,
because that doctor knows the
patient's history, etc. He said it
is a touch smaller so some of the
swelling it was creating has gone
down.

He said in January, 6 mos. after
the end of radiation, that it
should be dead. But he said it
won't actually show that way on
the MRI because all the cells are
dead inside but the mass just sits
there until hopefully the body
reabsorbs it at some
point...slowly I guess.

But the best news was I told him I
was getting zingers to my
face.....like a quick nerve
pain.....mostly lasting just a
split second, sometimes longer. He
was so excited to hear this. Told
me I made his day. It means the
nerves on the right side are still

alive and are starting to come
back.

So a great appointment. Several
times during the 30 min. he spent
with us he told me.....you've made
my day with the recovery you are
making!—T

Email Sent 1/28/2011

UCSF Appts. Today

I had appointments at UCSF today.
Visual field has improved
markedly. HUGE improvement.
And.....I got smarter. Had to do
the mental test again today for
two hours. She was most impressed
at how much better I did this time
than last time and how much
quicker I was at answering things.

So now we know the radiation did
NO damage to my brain function!—T

    I now felt like I wasn't ricocheting
as much through life. My balance was much
improved. If I'd been pulled over by a cop
and asked to walk a straight line, I still
couldn't do that, but I had no times now

where I felt like I might stumble and fall. I would sometimes veer to the left, or veer to the right, as I was walking.

Prior to working with Elizabeth, if someone had watched me walk down the street, they would have thought I was drunk. I veered off so often and rather starkly. It wasn't just a slow veering to the right; it was like BOOM and just BOOM! I'm over to the right, and then BOOM! I'm back to the left. This tendency has slowed down and now my veering is much more gradual. Not nearly as dramatic.

It's still hard for me to walk in a crowd though, because I can't really walk a straight line. I bump into people and bounce off of them. There is still a bit of ricocheting along. When this happens I'll sometimes get a look of annoyance. Other times they say, "Oops, sorry," like it was their fault. I like those folks better than the annoyed ones. I'm doing the best I can out here!

Chapter 18 Vision Solutions?

"Keep your face always toward the sunshine and shadows will fall behind you." —Walt Whitman

It was Marty Rossman that recommended I read something that Meir Schneider had written. He told me about his *School for Self Healing;* said he had met and heard Meir Schneider speak years ago and stated, "He's the real deal." He thought maybe Schneider could help with my right eyelid.

I went online, looked over all that Meir Schneider had written and figured the place to start was with a book about the story of his life.

Email sent on 4/18/2011

Am reading, to me, just a stunning book. My acupuncturist told me about this guy.....Meir Schneider. Just an amazing man. Was born with cataracts on his eyes. After many botches surgeries, he was blind at a very young age. He decided, as a child, that he was not going to be blind, so he did some research and trained his eyes to see. His whole family told him to stop it, it was a waste of time, etc. Only his grandmother encouraged him. Once he could see, he started to teach others. Then he started to heal people through massage and exercise......bad backs, arthritis, MS. It's just an amazing autobiography. Short read. Title is **Self-Healing. My life and vision by Meir Schneider.**

       Anyway, I was reading it last night while in bed and he's treating a lady (in Israel....that's where he grew up) for arthritis. She's in such pain that he can't even touch her. It just hurts her everywhere. So he tells her focus on your scalp. I'm thinking how clever, get her to focus away from her pain while he treats her. Later, when I'm starting to listen to my visualization tape and taking deep breaths, I start to cough. Lately I can only take one really deep breath and then the tickle returns and I have to take shallow breaths. So I think .....ok....focus on the scalp. I do that and the tickle goes completely away. Cool. So I continue to take really deep breaths. Next thing I know, my right nostril opens up. It has opened up a couple of times since surgery for maybe a few hours.....maybe even a whole day and then closes back up again. So that's cool it's open but not shocking.

Then Don asks me something, not realizing I have the headphones in. I answer and my voice is very different from when I went to bed. Lately, when I try and talk it vibrates in the back of my throat and causes me to cough. No more vibration. I'm pretty shocked when I hear my voice.....much, much stronger voice.

So I return to listening, breathing and relaxing, and each time I take a really deep breath, the whole right side of my head is filled with nerve ending sensations.....zingers, tingling, etc. After about 5 min. of this continually going on, I notice my jaw seems funny. I close my teeth and they slide into place. I actually can't believe this so I open and close my mouth several times and each time they slide into place. For the first time since the surgeries, my teeth are aligned.

I sit bolt upright....tell Don. I'm so excited. Am thinking no way am I going to be able to sleep. I'm going to lie here all night,

thinking about my scalp and taking
deep breaths.

This morning, all is in place. My
right nostril is open and my teeth
touch and then slide into place.
Before, my jaw would not slide at
all. Where ever the teeth came
down, that's where they stayed. I
could not slide them one way or
another.

Besides the book, I bought his CD
on how to train the eyes to see.
Not exactly my problem but maybe I
can train the double vision out of
the right eye and improve the
eyesight in that eye so that the
eye is more viable. Right now UCSF
considers it not even worth
working with because I can't read
enough of the eye chart.

Quite the evening here. I really,
really recommend the book to
everyone. He's been doing this
stuff ever since he was a kid. I
was completely inspired by the guy
20 pages into the book. What an
amazing individual. Midway through
his career he moved to SF and he
has a healing center in
SF...http://www.self-healing.org/.

After finishing Meir's book, I looked up the School of Self Healing and called them, asking for an appointment for treatment. The secretary asked, "Do you want to see Meir Schneider or one of his associates?" I was stunned. It had never occurred to me that he was seeing patients. Are you kidding? If I could actually meet and be treated by the amazing man in the book I'd just read, then yes of course I wanted to see Meir.

So I booked a two-hour session with Meir Schneider. I figured if I only booked an hour, it would take most of that time to explain how I had an eye in this condition.

I worked with Meir for about six months. From the beginning he said I'm not sure if I will be able to help you but we can certainly try. He felt, and I knew, that if had I found him sooner after surgery when I still had muscle strength in that eyelid, he'd have had a better chance of reactivating it. But on the Meir Schneider journey I went.

His strategy seemed to be: shake up the brain and what it considered normal to see if other areas of the brain fired up. One of the first things he had me do was go out into the backyard of the school and climb onto the trampoline. Wow, that was crazy for me. At first I was on my hands and knees, afraid to stand up. I barely had the stability to stand and walk down the street, let alone try and stand on this thing and actually move around.

But I knew from Meir's book that he was a very persistent guy, and working with him was a team effort. As half of this team, it was now my job to stand up and walk around the trampoline in the backyard of the School for Self-Healing.

I did it, very slowly and very carefully. One of his assistants came onto the surface with me, took both my hands and we did little baby jumps. My feet never left the surface. We were just making the surface go up and down a bit with him holding my hands to steady me so I could do it.

Six months later, after I ended treatments, I was able to stand and actually jump on the trampoline by myself. I had not been on it in months and was blown away by how very much my balance had improved. This time my feet actually did leave the surface! I have now purchased a mini-trampoline that sits in my back yard. I step on it several times a week as I walk through our yard, just to keep the brain sparking and realizing that all surfaces are not created equal!

Meir is an amazing man and friend. I highly recommend any of his Vision books. If you live in or travel to the San Francisco Bay area, make an appointment. Using a technique he calls the Bates Method of sunning and palming, he took my mother's glaucoma number from 23 to 16. She's still working on getting it lower. Her ophthalmologist was stunned. Even when she explained these methods, he wasn't a believer and told her the number must have gone down for some other reason.

I was in a unique position with the sunning and palming. With nerve endings on

the right side of my face still continuing
to try to re-connect, I often felt
fuzziness in and around my right eye area.
But while sunning, those nerve endings were
activated and the fuzziness always
intensified. It stayed intensified for two-
three hours after the sunning and palming.
I've asked my mom if she felt this too when
she suns, and she does not. I know it's
unique to me and a result of my surgeries.
I'm sure I'm one of the few people that can
actually feel the sunning and palming
working while I'm doing it.

Chapter 19 Balance Solutions

While I was working with Meir Schneider, I started going to a Sunday morning yoga class at my gym, Body Kinetics. Jasen and Allison, my son and daughter-in-law, as well as Allison's mother, had been telling me for a couple of years (pre-surgery) to do yoga. I was not against it; I just hadn't taken the time to get to classes. I started with a beginning yoga class with Beth Kraft.

Before the class I explained to her about my surgeries and how bad my balance was, although improving. She said that in the past year she had worked with a friend of hers that had also been through brain tumor surgery. Well, how perfect was that? Now I had a yoga instructor that completely understood my situation.

I thought I knew how bad my balance was but I had no clue until my first yoga class. Near the end of the class, we were on our knees and when we had to lift up one leg and put down that foot. That left us with one knee down and one foot down. I fell over. I was stunned. This was such a basic thing to do and I couldn't even stay upright in a simple pose.

I continued with weekly yoga sessions. It was quite the experience. I had no idea that I was walking and standing without being centered over my feet. I started concentrating in class, making sure that I stayed centered and balanced. That alone had made a HUGE difference.

I am also delighted that Beth showed us alternative stances if the pose was too challenging. I could not have discovered a better yoga class for me, or a better teacher. I continue to be astounded with how much yoga has helped me get my 'normal' back.

One day near the end of class, as I was standing straight up from having been bent over at the waist, I felt a rolling sensation at the base of my spinal column. It was very distinctive. It felt very round, about the size of a tennis ball. It rolled slowly up my spine and stopped at the base of my neck. I had no idea what it was. It created no other sensations in my body. Nothing seemed to get worse or to get better. It was pretty amazing to have such a distinctive feeling. In talking with Beth, we both think it was energy moving up my spine. Because the tumor had grown so large and pushed my brain stem to the side a bit, Beth and I had a hunch that maybe ganglia in my neck and spine had become a little compressed. The rolling sensation of energy may have been those ganglia loosening up a bit. Quite the experience.

Another class that was huge for me at Body Kinetics was the core muscle class by Roberta Kralj. This class helped with both my balance and by freeing up and loosening muscles that have been crunched together since the surgeries. I can definitely tell in my body when I miss a class. The muscles around my diaphragm start to tighten up, causing pain when I eat. While doing jumping jacks one day in class, I realized that when I raised my right arm over my head, it pulled the right side of my face with it. The whole right side of my face would just jerk to the right. After working and stretching all my different muscles in class, I can now do jumping jacks and my face stays in place.

In March, 2013, Roberta had us drape our body backward over an exercise ball. I was instantly on high alert. My body almost always felt so tight that I wasn't sure I should do this. I looked at the people to my right and they were all doing it, so I gathered that this was something the body could do. I tried. But my neck was still a little too stiff to completely relax down the ball and have the top of my head facing the floor.

The next morning I woke up with a strange feeling in my throat. I was breathing air into an area of my throat that had not felt incoming air from my nostril in three years. Crazy. Now I drape my body over my ottoman at least once a day to keep these muscles continually stretched out.

In the fall of 2012, Jasen, my son, and I were in Berkeley at a shoe store that used to be one of his accounts when he carried a shoe line. He chatted with the owner while I poked around looking at tennis shoes. I had worn the same brand of shoe every day since my surgeries and still had fuzzy feet periodically for what seemed like no particular reason.

Jasen looked up and said, "Mom, why don't you try high tops? They might give you more stability."

That made sense to me so I got two pairs. I took them home and put in my Super Feet shoe inserts. Jasen suggested I take them back out as they weren't letting my feet experience whatever surface I was walking on. That also made sense, so out they came.

The shoes were a *huge* turning point. My balance got even better. I wasn't wobbly at all and rarely got fuzzy feet. The problem was almost solved, except now as my grandchildren grew up and got married, I'd have to tell them Grandma will be wearing high tops to your wedding.

I tried wearing my old tennis shoes one day, and the high tops the next, then a different pair of shoes another day. I found this left me completely off balance and almost disoriented. My brain felt scrambled and it was hard to concentrate. It seemed clear that my various shoes affected the alignment of my spine, or brain stem, or something like that, and was completely throwing me off.

Back to only wearing high tops I went. A couple of times I tried varying the shoe choices again, but always with the same result. I've stopped playing around with shoes. It was completely exhausting to my brain and body to play shoe scramble. High tops are here to stay.

Chapter 20 Flossing in the Dark

"Make each day your masterpiece" —John Wooden

The date was October 26th, 2011. Amazing! After getting all the major things taken care of, the surgery and the radiation, I started nibbling away at balance through yoga and acupuncture.

Another thing on my list was to get back feeling in my jaw. When I flossed, it was as if I was flossing in the dark. I had no feeling in my teeth on the right side. My jaw was so misaligned that originally after the surgeries, my smile wasn't just a crooked smile; my whole lower jaw just fell drastically off to the right. My smile was completely lopsided. That did improve some on its own, but my teeth were not aligned, and I wasn't able to actually chew or grind food. I couldn't eat anything like steak or pork, because I couldn't grind it small enough to swallow it. In trying, I had started to get an odd wear on my teeth. However, my dentist had no suggestions for how I could improve this since he'd never come across anyone with my issues.

Everybody, my dentist, my doctors, Don, was concerned about what would happen to my teeth if they didn't line up. I could have them ground down to make them align, but because I could feel the nerve endings trying to connect still, my dentist felt we ought to leave my jaw alone and see what happened. Maybe as feeling came back, they would line up. I just hoped my teeth lasted long enough until we decided what to do.

Finally, when no help seemed to be coming from any of my professional contacts, I decided to go to the dental department at UCSF, and see if they had a specialist I could consult. Don thought this was a waste of my time and wanted to know what I thought I might accomplish with this visit. During some of my excursions with unknown practitioners, such as Meir Schneider, I had had no idea what I might accomplish. I wanted to add a person to my team of *practitioners*, or cross them off and move on.

Dr. Barani's office, my radiologist/oncologist recommended that I start with a Dr. White. He was very well known in the dental department. Dr. White was a hoot. He took one look at the misalignment of my mouth and jaw, and said, "You don't need to see me, you need to see Dr. Octavia Plesh. She's the specialist here who can build you something to wear in your mouth at night. Then your teeth can start realigning." I had thought maybe something like that might help but didn't really know if it would work for me or not.

He led me right over to Dr. Plesh, and asked her if she could see me right then. Don was with me. We sat down and explained to her what had happened with the surgeries.

She felt that with exercise I could still get my teeth to realign because my jaw was not locked into place. I could move it and push it around using my hand on the outside of the cheek. Perhaps a tens unit could also help. A tens unit gives off a little tiny electrical impulse that sparks the muscles and gets them back into use by

relaxing them. She gave me four exercises.
I started doing them three times a day;
morning, noon, and night.

In the meantime, I experienced some
feeling coming back into my teeth, slowly,
slowly, slowly. After doing the exercises
for three or four months, I was reading
email at my desk one day, and I experienced
what I could best describe as an earthquake
in my head. There was a feeling like
something had shifted on the right side,
and I literally had to sit back and take
stock: Was I still here? Could I still
think? Could I still process? It was such a
noticeable shift that to this day I don't
know what happened. I just call it an
earthquake in my head. It did, however,
leave me feeling weak and disoriented.

I was able to stand up and walk
around, but I had an art festival in two
days. I considered making the best of it
but ultimately thought, "I can't set up my
booth. If anyone asks me a question, I'm
not sure I can answer it. It seems too much
to try and have a conversation with
someone." So I called and cancelled.

My head earthquake happened a second in late 2012. I was walking into a doctor's appointment. My balance was instantly off, felt disoriented again. Don was walking with me and noticed it right away and asked if I was okay. Nope. I just had another earthquake in my head. But I kept walking as I now knew it was seemingly okay.

I could tell after the first head earthquake that the shift in the right side needed to happen. It aligned the teeth on the left side of my jaw, but it did not the right side or the front. I had no idea how my jaw could be jerked into that kind of position, but it seemed to have happened. At least I had my left side aligned for the moment. I didn't know if it was going to hold or not.

I immediately emailed Dr. Plesh and told her about the earthquake in my head and how the teeth on my left side now seemed to be aligned. "So, was this all okay? I seem to be mentally a little disoriented, and physically way off balance." I got an email right back, "Toni,

Toni, this is awesome news, this is
fabulous. Your jaw is starting to line back
up; this is wonderful."

My initial thought was, "This is
wonderful!? If you say so, though it feels
really odd, not wonderful." Within a
couple of days the disoriented feeling left
and my balance came back as good as it had
been. I seemed to be back on track. I felt
really bad that I had cancelled the art
festival, because by the time the art
festival actually happened I probably would
have been able to do it.

I continued on with Dr. Plesh's
exercises, and occasionally with the tens
unit. To use the tens unit, I had to put
little sticky pads on my face, which meant
sitting very still. If I moved around, the
pads would start to slip, or fall off. So I
didn't use the tens unit very often during
the process of realignment.

I stuck with the exercises that she
recommended. Gradually the right outside
edge of my teeth became aligned, but the
inside edge was still far apart. I could

almost fit my little finger tip in the gap. I couldn't gnaw or grind food, except on the left side.

At this point, Dr. Plesh suggested that I start chewing more on the right side and less on the left where the teeth were lined up. She wanted to strengthen the weaker muscles. I gave it a shot, but there wasn't enough tooth surfaces to chew and grind food. Also, that position caused the muscles at the back and base of my tongue to spasm. That was extremely painful. The muscle at the base of the tongue just clamps down and whoa! My subconscious tendency was to chew on the left side, and I had to remind myself to switch. At one point I asked Dr. Plesh if chewing gum would help, but she didn't want that much exercise going on.

She was concerned from the start that I not over exercise the right side as I could damage the muscle and need to start all over again. She reminded me, "This is going to be a slow, steady race. Just do a little bit at a time and we'll gradually get your jaw sliding back over."

One of the exercises Dr. Plesh had me
doing was pushing the left side of my face
with my fist to try and push the jaw over,
or I guess, pull the jaw over to meet that
pressure. Sometimes the next day, that
outside left area of my face hurt from
pushing so hard. I would then skip a day. I
wasn't doing the jaw pushes three times a
day every day, but more like once a day
because more than that overtaxed the
muscles on both sides of my face.

If I didn't do the exercises, I could
feel my jaw pulling back to the right. In
this instance I'd end up with a bit of a
lisp and the lower right area of my face
would be very tight. That was always a good
reminder. "Hey I haven't done the exercises
in a day or two; gotta get back at it."

One night I woke up and for the first
time in over three years, all of my teeth
were aligned.

Unfortunately my jaw didn't hold this
position, though it stayed aligned enough
that I could actually chew meat. I no
longer bit the side of my cheek or my

tongue, which was a big relief. I've bitten the side of my cheek so many times that I have a ridge of scar tissue on the inside.

I've kept up with the exercises because my muscles keep trying to pull back to the right, and probably will until my teeth and jaw realize this is the new normal—this is where they belong, this is where they're staying, and we're not going back to where we were before.

Once my muscles get used to this new position for a while, then the alignment should be permanent. The wear on my teeth can then go back to normal.

Some time later, the spasms at the back of my tongue returned, so I went in for a follow up appointment with one of my doctors. As I got out of the car my world was rocked again by the earthquake in my head. I felt completely off balance. Was I having a heart attack? I was disoriented, zigzagging all over the sidewalk, and back to ricocheting through life, as I say. But in the back of my mind I wondered if something was going on with my jaw, because of the tongue spasms. This time the spasms had occurred deeper than my tongue, way down in my throat. I finally decided that my jaw was just aligning again.

I was right. The next morning I woke up with my teeth aligned. Again, it took me a couple of days to feel less off balance, and reoriented in my life. Hopefully, this was another piece of my health puzzle solved, and I didn't have to take the puzzle pieces out again.

Chapter 21 Swallowing And Coughing

On one visit to Dr. Plesh, I mentioned I had great trouble swallowing and eating. My weight had stabilized and I was no longer losing ground. I had lost twenty pounds since my—surgeries so I was delighted to be able to hold my own weight-wise.

But as Don described, our meals always included drama. I would still have coughing spasms until I was breathless, and then end with a sneeze.

Dr. Plesh recommended a Dr. William Snape, Sutter Pacific Medical Center, a *neuro gastroenterologist*. Geez. Another neuro specialty. I was blown away that Dr. Plesh would reach out to her colleagues and find this doctor.

Don and I drove in for my initial appointment with Dr. Snape. We liked him from the start. Don had warned me before we went in that it was entirely possible there was nothing Dr. Snape could do for me.

Dr. Snape ordered a total of five tests. The first was a barium swallow. I had done this once already at Novato Hospital. At that time Don had watched as they'd performed the test and was stunned by what he saw. As you swallow, the esophagus should behave like a snake as the food or drink goes down. It compresses, moves the food along, compresses again, moves the food further down, etc. As we watched mine work, there was no compression going on. The swallow zinged from one side of my esophagus, then ricocheted back to the other side. We were amazed that I'd been able to get food down at all.

This redo of the test by Dr. Snape perhaps four months after the first one, showed the same results. The next day I went in for about five hours of testing. When I arrived, I had to eat a breakfast of scrambled eggs, toast and jam, orange juice and milk. Then I stood in front of the scanner so they could see how I was processing the food at it entered the body.

Next I was to wait in the waiting room for approximately two hours. Then I stood in front of the scanner again so they could see how far the food had progressed and if it had entered my stomach. I had several other scans throughout that day to see where and how long the food took to exit my stomach.

For one test I had a tube going down into my stomach. It was attached to a monitor so they could follow how my body was reacting to the food. This monitor was on for 24 hours.

Another day I had an endoscopy.

The results of all the tests determined that I had a fried stomach and a tortuous esophagus. Ugh! That didn't sound nice at all.

Having a fried stomach means that when Dr. Snape touched the side of my stomach during my endoscopy, it would bleed with just the lightest touch of the endoscope. Not something you want to have going on in your stomach.

A tortuous esophagus simply meant it was not functioning like a snake, but it certainly fit my ricocheting life. Also not a good thing.

My understanding of Dr. Snape's specialty is that he can go into the esophagus with an instrument and lightly shock the muscles to get them working again.

Unfortunately, he cannot do this when the damage to the esophagus was caused by a prior event like my surgeries. The surgeries had damaged the muscles so they simply did not work correctly any longer and there was nothing his magical instrument could do to fix them.

This was a bit depressing to me and before we walked back out to the car I was in tears. It seems that for the rest of my life I'd be coughing and having drama as I ate. Eventually I decided if that was the worst of it, I could deal. I was just so used to taking each challenge head on and finding a solution. This one was tough for me as it appeared there was no medical solution. At least not until modern medicine caught up with me.

Dr. Snape did prescribe two medications that have literally changed my life. Don describes it as "We no longer have drama at each meal." I am able to eat now without the coughing and gagging going on. It was truly a remarkable difference. My path crossing with Dr. Snape's has been life changing. The medicines coat the esophagus and allow food to slide down easier.

In the fall of 2011, I drove up to Lake Tahoe with my mother and stepfather, George, for a small family reunion. Jasen, Allison and Austen were coming in from Portland. My younger brother Kelly and his wife Nancy were coming in from Atlanta. And my Uncle Ed (my mom's brother) and his daughter Louann were coming from Arizona.

We did this again in the fall of 2012.

While at Lake Tahoe, each time after eating, I promptly got sick and vomited, or at least attempted to. In the fall of 2011, I was unable to vomit. It got stuck and I instantly was unable to breath. Not knowing what to do (it was the middle of the night

and everyone was asleep), I swallowed the
vomit. As soon as it hit my stomach, it
came back up again and this time I could
vomit. Everyone agreed that I probably had
food poisoning from the restaurant where we
had dinner. I'd had food poisoning before
and this was not accompanied by the severe
stomach cramps that I had experienced with
food poisoning. It was still the best guess
that anyone had.

In the fall of 2012, after dinner the
first night I again went into my room to
vomit. This time I was able to vomit
successfully. To me, this in and of itself
was a huge improvement. Jasen texted
immediately (as they were not able to
attend this reunion): "you have altitude
sickness". Really? I'd never had that in my
life and I'd lived in Albuquerque, NM for
12 years at a mile high.

I could only figure that this was
somehow a result of my brain being altered
a bit and now I got altitude sickness.
People have since told me that if I want to
go to a higher altitude, stop about half
way up to that height, hang out, have

lunch, and let the body acclimate a bit. Then continue on to my destination. They said when they've done this they no longer experience altitude sickness.

In 2012 and 2013, I'd taken my grandson Luke up to Portland to visit his Aunt, Uncle and two cousins. With the help of Jasen and Allison, I took Luke and his cousin George to Mt. Hood to learn to snowboard. I stayed in the condo and the kids enjoyed the snow. In 2012 there was no problem with me at this altitude but Jasen told me that we are at about half the altitude that I was at Lake Tahoe.

So in Feb., 2013, we arrived at our condo at Mt. Hood and I had a constant cough going on, probably every ten minutes or so. By the next day it had gotten more frequent. By now Jasen had noticed and was worried. We ran a humidifier in my bedroom that night thinking maybe it was just too dry on the mountain for me.

They came back from snowboarding that second day and even though we had reserved the condo for that night, Jasen suggested we go back to Portland. All we were doing was spending the night and going back the next morning anyway. He wanted to get me back to civilization and near medical centers in case that became important.

We returned to their house and went to bed. In the middle of the night, I awoke unable to breath. It felt like my entire throat was drastically twisted sideways. Trying not to panic, I kept thinking just calm down, you'll sneeze shortly and be able to breath. I could feel a small space in the throat that seemed like I could get a tiny amount of air through. I focused on that and pictured it in my head and tried to relax and get my throat to untwist.

Didn't work. At this point I became concerned that I might black out or die. I was just about to roll out of bed and crawl down to Jasen and Allison's room when suddenly it untwisted and I gasped in huge amounts of air.

I had appointments in Portland the next day with David Tircuit for acupuncture, followed by Aki for a shiatsu massage. I explained to each what had happened and both said: You got cold and the muscles all clamped down in one big spasm. But I wasn't even outside I protested. Didn't matter they both said. You looked outside, saw all the snow and a shiver went up your spine. Sure. That happens to everyone when you live in a cold climate and look outside. That's all it took they said. You didn't have to physically get cold. You just had to see the cold.

A week later I had a follow up appointment with Dr. Snape and he said it sounded like I had a tracheal spasm. From what I described, it wasn't my esophagus but my trachea. He said I had cold-induced asthma and recommended I keep an inhaler with me at all times, which I now do.

For me, I'm done with anything much above sea level. Safer down here for me it seems. That was a frightening experience.

1/23/2013 Email to friends/family.

Latest MRI scan done on 1/16/2013 came back showing no tumor growth among the pieces left in my brain.

On Jan. 23rd we met with Dr. Barani, my oncologist, so he could report these results to us. He also declared me 'cured'.

He said when we have a patient that is at least three years post-surgery (I am now three and a half years post) with no visible tumor growth, we declare you 'cured'. Clearly the tumor had not morphed into something faster growing so they expect after three years that there will be no new changes in the pattern of the tumor.

He advised me to, "Go out there and get on with life. You no longer have this hanging over your head. Go forth and travel the world!"

Most fabulous news I'd heard in a long time!

"Impossible is a word only to be found in the dictionary of fools." —Napoleon

Email received from my long-time friend Carole Marchette:

Hey girlfriend,

I've been thinking about all the magnificent men and women you have attracted to your life and healing process lately. I am truly in awe of your pluck, determination and courage. Over the last 30 or so years, you have become a role model for me (and many others), I'm sure. So now when I'm faced with any adversity, I think of you, Toni. As a woman, a wife, a mother, grandmother and my sister-of-the-heart (the very best kind to have)... you gently touch so many lives. I just want to say thank you.

Carole Marchette

Received on 9/23/2011 from Carole

I've read about women (in fiction) who have pluck, stamina, determination, courage, smarts, beauty and a loving spirit. You, girlfriend, are the real deal!!!!!!!!!!!!Thanx. Carole

"Think where man's glory most begins and ends, and say my glory was I had such friends." W.B. Yeats

Thanks to one and all that were, and
continue to be, part of Team Toni! My
healing will continue.

Chapter 22 Catching Up

So where am I now, four-plus years post surgeries?

It is rare for me to feel off balance. If I miss too many yoga classes or my core exercise class at Body Kinetics, my balance will start to be off again. It appears these will be life-long classes for me.

The hearing in my right ear is about 80%. I can hear on the telephone and also my iPhone using that ear. At this point, it seems that might be as good as it gets. It's difficult for me to hear if someone is speaking to me from another room. It sounds very garbled. But otherwise, it's not really an issue.

My right eyelid remains closed. I continue to exercise it using my fingers. I also continue with the sunning and palming that Meir Schneider taught me. There is still no feeling in my eyeball. But I do still have nerves trying to connect and there is some muscle twitching in and around the eye socket area. However, this year my *neuro ophthalmologist*, Dr. Hoyt at UCSF, said there is no need for me to come back unless there is some change in my eye or eyelid.

Don and I did go into UCSF to see a new vision specialist that had just joined the UCSF team. Dr. Hoyt recommended him, saying he was doing things that were new to all of them.

Dr. Kersten spoke with us and examined my eye. He wanted to attach the eyelid to my eyebrow so I would lift my eyebrow to open my eye.

I asked if he knew that I had no feeling in my eyeball. No. He was not aware of that.

In that case, he suggested neither he nor I would be happy if he attached the eyelid to the eyebrow. He said the cornea would receive too much light and would be damaged. Both Don and I had great respect for his credentials and opinion so for now, my eyelid does not open. I've run through all available options and will wait for medicine to catch up with me to create a fix.

My voice is strong. Eating has become a joy again since seeing Dr. Snape and getting on the meds he prescribed. There is no more drama at mealtime. Maybe once or twice a week, I'll have a bit of coughing. Nothing like the coughing spasms I had before.

It seems I do have altitude sickness now. Something I never had before. I also have cold induced asthma. I now carry an inhaler with me should my trachea ever spasm again as it did in Portland in February, 2013.

My teeth are so close to being lined up that I rarely notice they are off by a hair. I can eat any food that comes my way, either because they lined up or because I've learned a work around. My jaw does still move around just a touch. I'm pretty sure it's a work in progress.

In October, 2013, I was notified that my health insurance was being cancelled. My health insurance company, HealthNet, had been amazing during my surgeries and many bills. It was completely seamless. I never heard from them. Never had to call them. Bills came in and they paid the bills.

The Affordable Care Act (ACA or Obamacare) decided my plan was not acceptable under the new health care law.

It became a full time job finding a health plan. A health plan that would include UCSF and also all my specialists at UCSF. I was unwilling to neither change from UCSF nor trade in my docs. I'm still not sure I found that plan and won't know until UCSF bills the insurance for visits in February, 2014.

In November, 2013, one last issue was solved. For about two months, every two weeks or so, I would wake up in the middle of the night with my toes cramped up. The first time it happened it was just one foot. The last time it happened it was both feet. On previous occasions, I had been able to reach down, wiggle them around for a while, and they would uncramp. The last time, when it was both feet, I could not

get them to uncramp. I finally got out of
bed and walked around until they un-
cramped.

Everyone I told about it had the same
reaction. "Really, they cramped *up*?" Yes,
up.

In November I was in Portland again
and mentioned it to David Tircuit, thinking
maybe it was something acupuncture could
address. His reaction was the same as
others. "Really? Up?" But in went the
needles and again David solved this problem
as well as a problem that had been nagging
me since my surgeries.

Part of the original reason for seeing
Dr. Snape about eating issues was that I
had a constant pain in my left stomach
area. Even as I was doing Dr. Snape's
tests, the pain was there. The medication
he put me on allowed me to eat without the
coughing and gagging but did nothing to
alleviate my stomach pain.

One day I reached up to hold on to the
door frame in our kitchen to stretch out
muscles. Wow. Away went the pain. I did it

again the next day. The pain went away again. I now knew this was a muscle issue.

On the day that David put the needles in to stop the toe cramping, he also un-cramped this stomach muscle. The stomach muscle was apparently reaching down and grabbing my toes at night while I slept. With the acupuncture treatment he did, both problems are now solved. It is unbelievable to me that my pain is finally gone after four years.

In December, 2013 I met my new neurosurgeon. Dr. Parsa left to be Department Head at Northwestern. My new doctor was the Department Head at UCSF, Dr. McDermott. He decided it was time to run a blood test to make sure, with all the radiation I had, that the pituitary was functioning fine.

The test came back slightly high so he ordered another blood test. Again the results were just out of the normal range.

Dr. McDermott felt it was now time I see a pituitary specialist. I was referred to Dr. Blevins. He is a Neuro

Endocrinologist. Long blood tests ordered this time. One of them with samples taken every 30 minutes for 4 hours.

The result is that I am basically producing dismal amounts of human growth hormone (HGH). I didn't realize adults needed it. It regulates bone density, cholesterol, weight, memory and a host of other things.

The recommendation—begin HGH shots. A daily shot that I administer myself. Started out with a low dose until I got to the dosage I needed for my body.

The best guess is that the radiation I received killed this function of the pituitary gland. This is a common result for patients who have received radiation therapy.

I am a work in progress. My major hurdles since surgery have now been addressed. I simply need to continue on my boat and keep sailing along!

Let me finish with this quote:

"This is the true joy of life, the being used for a purpose recognized by yourself is a mighty one; the being a force of nature instead of a feverish, selfish little clod of ailments and grievances complaining that the world will not devote itself to making you happy.

I am of the opinion that my life belongs to the whole community, and as long as I live it is my privilege to do for it whatever I can. I want to be thoroughly used up when I die for the harder I work the more I live.

I rejoice in life for its own sake. Life is no 'brief candle' for me. It is a sort of splendid torch, which I have got hold of for the moment, and I want to make it burn as brightly as possible before handing it on to future generations." —George Bernard Shaw

Made in the USA
San Bernardino, CA
25 May 2014